Numerical Computing with IEEE Floating Point Arithmetic

Numerical Computing with IEEE Floating Point Arithmetic

Including One Theorem, One Rule of Thumb, and One Hundred and One Exercises

Michael L. Overton
Courant Institute of Mathematical Sciences
New York University
New York, New York

Society for Industrial and Applied Mathematics
Philadelphia

Copyright © 2001 by the Society for Industrial and Applied Mathematics.

10 9 8 7 6 5 4 3 2

All rights reserved. Printed in the United States of America. No part of this book may be reproduced, stored, or transmitted in any manner without the written permission of the publisher. For information, write to the Society for Industrial and Applied Mathematics, 3600 University City Science Center, Philadelphia, PA 19104-2688.

Library of Congress Cataloging-in-Publication Data

Overton, Michael L.
  Numerical computing with IEEE floating point arithmetic / Michael L. Overton.
    p. cm.
  Includes bibliographical references and index.
  ISBN 0-89871-571-7
    1. Computer arithmetic. 2. Floating-point arithmetic. 3. Numerical calculations.
    I. Title.

QA76.9.M35 O94 2001
004'.01'51--dc21

00-067941

 is a registered trademark.

Dedicated to girls who like math
especially my daughter
Eleuthera Overton Sa

Contents

Preface	ix
Acknowledgments	xi
1 Introduction	1
2 The Real Numbers	5
3 Computer Representation of Numbers	9
4 IEEE Floating Point Representation	17
5 Rounding	25
6 Correctly Rounded Floating Point Operations	31
7 Exceptions	41
8 The Intel Microprocessors	49
9 Programming Languages	55
10 Floating Point in C	59
11 Cancellation	71
12 Conditioning of Problems	77
13 Stability of Algorithms	83
14 Conclusion	97
Bibliography	101

Preface

Numerical computing is a vital part of the modern scientific infrastructure. Almost all numerical computing uses floating point arithmetic, and almost every modern computer implements the IEEE[1] binary floating point standard, published in 1985. This standard is arguably the most important in the computer industry, the result of an unprecedented cooperation between academic computer scientists and the cutting edge of industry. Nonetheless, many years after its publication, the key ideas of the IEEE standard remain poorly understood by many students and computer professionals. Perhaps this is because an easily accessible yet reasonably detailed discussion of the standard has not been available—hence, the evolution of this short book. Although it is intended primarily for computer science or mathematics students, as a supplement to a more traditional textbook for a course in scientific computing, numerical analysis, or computer architecture, it also aims to reach a broader audience. As well as the IEEE standard, topics include the floating point architecture of the Intel microprocessors, a discussion of programming language support for the standard, and an introduction to the key concepts of cancellation, conditioning, and stability. The book should be accessible to any reader with an interest in computers and mathematics. Some basic knowledge of calculus and programming is assumed in the second half. The style is not that of a traditional textbook. There is enough variety of content that all but the most expert readers will find something of interest here.

A web page for the book is maintained at

> http://www.cs.nyu.edu/cs/faculty/overton/book/

Refer to this page for corrections to the text, to download programs from the book, and to link to the web pages mentioned in the bibliography, which will be updated as necessary.

MICHAEL L. OVERTON

---

[1] Institute for Electrical and Electronics Engineers. IEEE is pronounced "I triple E."

Acknowledgments

Special thanks go to Jim Demmel for introducing me to the IEEE floating point standard years ago, answering many questions, and encouraging me to complete this work. Thanks also to Vel Kahan, without whom we would not have the standard, and to Chris Paige, who taught from an early version of this book and made many helpful suggestions. I am also grateful to many other people for their detailed comments, particularly David Gay, David Goldberg, Ilse Ipsen, Jorge Nocedal, Nick Trefethen, and Margaret Wright. Being part of a network of colleagues like these is the greatest pleasure of my professional life. I particularly thank Gene Golub and Olof Widlund for their crucial support during my early postdoctoral research career; I would not have been able to begin this work without them. Thanks also to Joe Darcy, Nick Higham, David Scott and Antoine Trux for pointing out errors in the first printing that are corrected in this second printing.

Many thanks to Vickie Kearn for her enthusiasm for publishing this book despite its unconventional format, to Beth Gallagher for her careful copy editing, and to all those involved in the production process. The publication of this book is one of many rewarding aspects of my association with SIAM during the past decade.

On a more personal note, I honor the memory of my father, David, who continues to inspire me many years after his passing, and I especially thank three wonderful people: my mother Kathie, my daughter Eleuthera, and my best friend Renan.

> Accurate reckoning: The entrance into knowledge
> of all existing things and all obscure secrets
>
> — A'HMOSÈ, *The Rhind Mathematical Papyrus*, c. 1650 B.C.

> I am a HAL Nine Thousand computer Production Number 3. I became
> operational at the Hal Plant in Urbana, Illinois, on January 12, 1997.
> The quick brown fox jumps over the lazy dog.
> The rain in Spain is mainly in the plain.
> Dave—are you still there?
> Did you know that the square root of 10 is 3.162277660168379?
> Log 10 to the base e is 0.434294481903252 ...
> correction, that is log e to the base 10 ...
> The reciprocal of 3 is 0.333333333333333333333 ...
> 2 times 2 is ... 2 times 2 is ...
> approximately 4.101010101010101010 ...
> I seem to be having difficulty ...
>
> —HAL, in *2001: A Space Odyssey*

Chapter 1

Introduction

Numerical computing means *computing with numbers*, and the subject is almost as old as civilization itself. Ancient peoples knew techniques to carry out many numerical tasks. Among the oldest computational records that we have is the Egyptian Rhind Papyrus from about 1650 B.C. [Cha79], quoted on the previous page. Counting stones and counting rods have been used for calculation for thousands of years; the abacus originated as a flat surface with counting stones and was used extensively in the ancient world long before it evolved into the device with beads on wires that was common in Asia until recently. The abacus was the basis of calculation in Europe until the introduction of our familiar positional decimal notation from the Middle East, beginning in the 13th century. By the end of the 16th century, positional decimal notation was in standard use throughout Europe, as it became widely recognized for its computational convenience.

The next key development was the invention and tabulation of logarithms by John Napier at the beginning of the 17th century; his idea was that time-consuming multiplication and especially division may be avoided by adding or subtracting logarithms, using tabulated values. Isaac Newton laid the foundations of modern numerical computing later in the 17th century, developing numerical techniques for the solution of many mathematical problems and inventing calculus along the way. Several of Newton's computational methods still bear his name. In Newton's footsteps followed Euler, Lagrange, Gauss, and many other great mathematicians of the 18th and 19th centuries.

The idea of using physical devices as an aid to calculation is an old one. The abacus has already been mentioned. The slide rule was invented soon after Napier's discovery of logarithms, although it was not commonly used until the middle of the 19th century. Numbers are represented on a slide rule explicitly in a logarithmic scale, and its moving rule and cursor allow multiplication and division to be carried out easily, accurate to about three decimal digits. This simple, inexpensive device was used by many generations of engineers and remained in common use until about 1975, when it was made obsolete by cheap electronic calculators. Mechanical calculating machines were devised by Schickard, Pascal, and Leibnitz in the 17th century; their descendants also remained in use until about 1975. The idea of a programmable machine that would operate without human intervention was developed in great depth by Charles Babbage in the 19th century, but his ideas were way ahead of his time and were mostly ignored. During World War II, scientific laboratories had rooms full of people doing different parts of a complicated calculation using pencil and paper, slide rules, and mechanical calculators. At that time, the word *computer* referred to a person, and those group calculations may be viewed as the early steps of parallel computing.

The Computer Age

The machine often described as the world's first operating computer was the Z3, built by the engineer Konrad Zuse in Germany in 1939–1941. The Z3 used electromechanical switching devices and computed with binary floating point numbers, a concept to be described in detail in subsequent chapters.[2] Although Zuse developed his machines during World War II, his government took no interest in his work. Slightly later, and in great secrecy, the British government developed a powerful electronic code-breaking machine, the Colossus. The first general-purpose operational electronic computer[3] is usually said to be the ENIAC (Electronic Numerical Integrator And Computer), a decimal machine with 18,000 vacuum tubes that was built by Eckert and Mauchly at the University of Pennsylvania in 1943–1945. Eckert was the electronics expert and Mauchly had the experience with extensive numerical computations. The intellectual giants who most influenced the postwar computer design in England and the United States were Alan Turing, one of the architects of the Colossus project, and John von Neumann, the Hungarian mathematician at Princeton. Two ideas in particular were advocated by von Neumann: the storage of instructions in the memory of the computer and the use of binary rather than decimal storage and arithmetic. The first fully functional stored-program electronic computers were built in England in 1948–1949; besides Turing, key leaders there included Maurice Wilkes and James Wilkinson. In the late 1940s and early 1950s, it was feared that the rounding errors inherent in floating point computing would make nontrivial calculations too inaccurate to be useful. Wilkinson demonstrated conclusively that this was not the case with his extensive computational experiments and innovative analysis of rounding errors accumulated in the course of a computation. Wilkinson's analysis was inspired by the work of Goldstine and von Neumann and of Turing [Wil64]. For more on the early history of computers, see [Wil85]. For a remarkable collection of essays by a cast of stars from the early days of computing, see [MHR80].

During the 1950s, the primary use of computers was for numerical computing in scientific applications. In the 1960s, computers became widely used by large businesses, but their purpose was not primarily numerical; instead, the principal use of computers became the processing of large quantities of information. Nonnumerical information, such as character strings, was represented in the computer using binary numbers, but the primary business applications were not numerical in nature. During the next three decades, computers became ever more widespread, becoming available to medium-sized businesses in the 1970s and to many millions of small businesses and individuals during the personal computer revolution of the 1980s and 1990s. The vast majority of these computer users do not see computing with numbers as their primary interest; instead, they are interested in the processing of information, such as text, images, and sound. Users are often not aware that manipulation of images and sound involves a lot of numerical computing.

Science Today

In scientific disciplines, numerical computing is essential. Physicists use computers to solve complicated equations modeling everything from the expansion of the universe to the microstructure of the atom, and to test their theories against experimental

---
[2]Ideas that seem to originate with Zuse include the hidden significand bit [Knu98, p. 227], to be discussed in Chapter 3, the use of ∞ and NaN [Kah96b], to be discussed in Chapter 7, the main ideas of algorithmic programming languages [Wil85, p. 225], and perhaps the concept of a stored program [Zus93, p. 44]. His autobiography [Zus93] gives an amazing account of his successful efforts at computer design and construction amid the chaos of World War II.

[3]A much more limited machine was developed a little earlier in Iowa.

data. Chemists and biologists use computers to determine the molecular structure of proteins. Medical researchers use computers for imaging techniques and for the statistical analysis of experimental and clinical observations. Atmospheric scientists use numerical computing to process huge quantities of data and to solve equations to predict the weather. Electronics engineers design ever faster, smaller, and more reliable computers using numerical simulation of electronic circuits. Modern airplane and spacecraft design depends heavily on computer modeling. Ironically, the tragic *Challenger* accident in January 1986 was due more to political errors than to scientific ones. From a scientific point of view, reentry of the space shuttle into the atmosphere was a far more delicate and difficult procedure than lift-off, and many nervous scientists were elated and relieved to see that their calculations had worked so well when the space shuttle first reentered the atmosphere and landed.

In brief, all fields of science and engineering rely heavily on numerical computing. The traditional two branches of science are theoretical science and experimental science. *Computational science* is now often mentioned as a third branch, having a status that is essentially equal to, perhaps even eclipsing, that of its two older siblings. The availability of greatly improved computational techniques and immensely faster computers allows the routine solution of complicated problems that would have seemed impossible just a generation ago.

Chapter 2

The Real Numbers

The *real* numbers can be represented conveniently by a line. Every point on the line corresponds to a real number, but only a few are marked in Figure 2.1. The line stretches infinitely far in both directions, towards ∞ and $-\infty$, which are not themselves numbers in the conventional sense but are included among the *extended real* numbers. The *integers* are the numbers $0, 1, -1, 2, -2, 3, -3, \ldots$. We say that there is an *infinite* but *countable* number of integers; by this we mean that every integer would eventually appear in the list if we count for long enough, even though we can never count all of them. The *rational* numbers are those that consist of a ratio of two integers, e.g., $1/2, 2/3, 6/3$; some of these, e.g., $6/3$, are integers. To see that the number of rational numbers is countable, imagine them listed in an infinite two-dimensional array as in Figure 2.2. Listing the first line and then the second, and so on, does not work, since the first line never terminates. Instead, we generate a list of all rational numbers diagonal by diagonal: first 0, then $\pm 1/1$; then $\pm 2/1, \pm 1/2$; then $\pm 3/1, \pm 2/2, \pm 1/3$; then $\pm 4/1, \pm 3/2, \pm 2/3, \pm 1/4$; etc. In this way, every rational number (including every integer) is eventually generated. In fact, every rational number is generated many times (e.g., $1/2$ and $2/4$ are the same number). However, every rational number does have a unique representation in lowest terms, achieved by canceling any common factor in the numerator and denominator (thus $2/4$ reduces to $1/2$).

The *irrational* numbers are the real numbers that are not rational. Familiar examples of irrational numbers are $\sqrt{2}, \pi$, and e. The numbers $\sqrt{2}$ and π have been studied for more than two thousand years. The number e, mentioned in the quote from HAL on page xiii, is the limit of
$$\left(1 + \frac{1}{n}\right)^n$$
as $n \to \infty$. Investigations leading to the definition of e began in the 17th century. Every irrational number can be defined as the limit of a sequence of rational numbers,

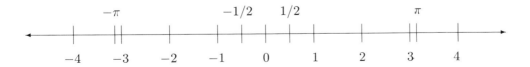

Figure 2.1: The Real Line

	1	2	3	4	...
1	±1/1	±1/2	±1/3	±1/4	...
2	±2/1	±2/2	±2/3	±2/4	...
3	±3/1	±3/2	±3/3	±3/4	...
4	±4/1	±4/2	±4/3	±4/4	...
...	...	...	...	...	...

Figure 2.2: The Nonzero Rational Numbers

but there is no way of listing all the irrational numbers—the set of irrational numbers is said to be *uncountable*.

Positional Number Systems

The idea of representing numbers using powers of 10 was used by many ancient peoples, e.g., the Hebrews, the Greeks, the Romans, and the Chinese, but the positional system we use today was not. The Romans used a system where each power of 10 required a different symbol: X for 10, C for $100 = 10^2$, M for $1000 = 10^3$, etc., and repetition, together with additional symbols for quinary groupings, was used to indicate how many of each power of 10 were present. For example, MDCCCCLXXXV means $1000 + 500 + 400 + 50 + 30 + 5 = 1985$. The familiar abbreviations such as IV for 4 were not used by the Romans. The Chinese system, which is still in use, is similar except that instead of repetition, symbols for the numbers 1 through 9 are used to modify each power of 10. These systems allowed easy transcription of numbers to an abacus for calculation, although they are not convenient for calculation with pencil and paper.

Large numbers cannot be conveniently represented by such systems. The positional notation used worldwide today requires a key idea: the representation of zero by a symbol. As far as we know, this was first used by the Babylonians about 300 B.C. Our decimal positional system was developed in India around 600 A.D. and was used for centuries by the Arabs in the Middle East before being passed on to Europe during the period 1200–1600—hence the name "Arabic numerals." This decimal, or base 10, system requires 10 symbols, representing the numbers 0 through 9. The system is called *positional* (or place-value) because the meaning of the number is understood from the position of the symbols, or *digits*, of the number. Zero is needed, for example, to distinguish 601 from 61. The reason for the decimal choice is the simple biological fact that humans have 10 fingers and thumbs. Indeed, the word *digit* derives from the Latin word for finger. Other positional systems developed by ancient peoples include the base 60 system used by the Babylonians, the vestiges of which are still seen today in our division of the hour into 60 minutes and the minute into 60 seconds, and the base 20 system developed by the Mayans, which was used for astronomical calculations. The Mayans are the only people known to have invented the positional number system, with its crucial use of a symbol for zero, independently of the Babylonians.

Decimal notation was initially used only for integers and was not used much for fractions until the 17th century. A reluctance to use decimal fractions is still evident in the use of quarters, eighths, sixteenths, etc., for machine tool sizes in the United States (and, until recently, for stock market prices).

Although decimal representation is convenient for people, it is not particularly convenient for use on computers. The binary, or base 2, system is much more useful: in this, every number is represented as a string of *bits*, each of which is either 0 or 1. The word *bit* is an abbreviation for *binary digit*; a *bitstring* is a string of bits. Each bit corresponds to a different power of 2, just as each digit of a decimal number corresponds to a different power of 10. Computer storage devices are all based on binary representation: the basic unit is also called a bit, which may be viewed as a single physical entity that is either "off" or "on." Bits in computer storage are organized in groups of 8, each called a *byte*. A byte can represent any of $256 = 2^8$ (2 to the power 8) different bitstrings, which may be viewed as representing the integers from 0 to 255. Alternatively, we may think of these 256 different bitstrings as representing 256 different *characters*.[4] A *word* is 4 consecutive bytes of computer storage (i.e., 32 bits), and a *double word* is 8 consecutive bytes (64 bits). A kilobyte is $1024 = 2^{10}$ bytes, a megabyte is 1024 kilobytes (2^{20} bytes), a gigabyte is 1024 megabytes (2^{30} bytes), a terabyte is 1024 gigabytes (2^{40} bytes), and a petabyte is 1024 terabytes (2^{50} bytes). Petabyte storage devices now exist, although they would have seemed almost unimaginably large just a decade ago. It is often useful to remember that 2^{10} is approximately 10^3. The Greek prefixes *kilo, mega, giga, tera*, and *peta* generally mean $10^3, 10^6, 10^9, 10^{12}$, and 10^{15}, respectively, in other scientific contexts, but with computers, powers of 2 are more important than powers of 10.

Although the binary system was not in wide use before the computer age, the idea of representing numbers as sums of powers of 2 is far from new. It was used as the basis for a multiplication algorithm described in the *Rhind Mathematical Papyrus* [Cha79], written nearly four millennia ago (see p. xiii).

Binary and Decimal Representation

Every real number has a decimal representation and a binary representation (and, indeed, a representation in a base equal to any integer greater than 1). Instead of representation, we sometimes use the word *expansion*. The representation of integers is straightforward, requiring an expansion in nonnegative powers of the base. For example, consider the number

$$(71)_{10} = 7 \times 10 + 1$$

and its binary equivalent

$$(1000111)_2 = 1 \times 64 + 0 \times 32 + 0 \times 16 + 0 \times 8 + 1 \times 4 + 1 \times 2 + 1 \times 1. \quad (2.1)$$

Nonintegral real numbers have digits (or bits) to the right of the decimal (or binary) point; these expansions may be finite or nonterminating. For example, 11/2 has the expansions

$$\frac{11}{2} = (5.5)_{10} = 5 \times 1 + 5 \times \frac{1}{10}$$

and

$$\frac{11}{2} = (101.1)_2 = 1 \times 4 + 0 \times 2 + 1 \times 1 + 1 \times \frac{1}{2}. \quad (2.2)$$

Both of these expansions terminate. However, the number 1/10, which obviously has

---

[4]The ASCII encoding scheme defines standard character interpretations for the first 128 of these bitstrings; Unicode is an extension that defines up to 2^{16} two-byte characters, allowing encoding of virtually all written languages in the world.

the finite decimal representation $(0.1)_{10}$, does not have a finite binary representation. Instead, it has the nonterminating expansion

$$\frac{1}{10} = (0.0001100110011\ldots)_2 = \frac{1}{16} + \frac{1}{32} + \frac{0}{64} + \frac{0}{128} + \frac{1}{256} + \frac{1}{512} + \frac{0}{1024} + \cdots. \quad (2.3)$$

Note that this representation, although nonterminating, is *repeating*. The fraction 1/3 has nonterminating expansions in both binary and decimal:

$$\frac{1}{3} = (0.333\ldots)_{10} = (0.010101\ldots)_2.$$

Rational numbers always have either finite or repeating expansions. For example,

$$\frac{1}{7} = (0.142857142857\ldots)_{10}.$$

In fact, any finite expansion can also be expressed as a repeating expansion. For example, 1/10 can be expressed as

$$\frac{1}{10} = (0.0999\ldots)_{10}.$$

However, we will use the finite expansion when it exists.

Irrational numbers always have nonterminating, nonrepeating expansions. For example,

$$\sqrt{2} = (1.414213\ldots)_{10}, \ \pi = (3.141592\ldots)_{10}, \ e = (2.71828182845\ldots)_{10}.$$

The first 10 digits of e may suggest that its representation is repeating, but it is not.

Exercise 2.1 *Conversion of integers from binary representation to decimal is straightforward, because we are so familiar with the decimal representations of the powers of 2. Devise (or recall) a systematic method to convert the decimal representation of an integer to binary. Which do you find more convenient: determining the bits from left to right, or from right to left? Both methods are acceptable, but once you get the idea, one of them is easier to use systematically than the other. Test your choice on some examples and convert the binary results back to decimal as a check. Does your method extend to convert a finite decimal representation of a nonintegral rational number, such as 0.1, to its binary representation?*

When working with binary numbers, many people prefer to use octal notation (base 8), using the symbols 0 through 7 to abbreviate the bitstrings 000 through 111. An alternative is the hexadecimal system (base 16), using the symbols 0,...,9,A,...,F to represent the bitstrings 0000 through 1111.

Chapter 3

Computer Representation of Numbers

What is the best way to represent numbers on the computer? Let us start by considering integers. Typically, integers are stored using a 32-bit word, so we confine our attention to this case. If we were concerned only with nonnegative integers, the representation would be easy: a bitstring specifying the binary representation of the integer. For example, the integer 71 (see (2.1)) would be stored as

$$\boxed{00000000000000000000000001000111}.$$

The nonnegative integers that we can represent in this way range from 0 (a bitstring of 32 zeros) to $2^{32} - 1$ (a bitstring of 32 ones). The number 2^{32} is too big, since its binary representation consists of a one followed by 32 zeros.

Signed Integers via 2's Complement

In fact, we need to be able to represent negative integers in addition to positive integers and 0. The most obvious idea is *sign-and-modulus*: use one of the 32 bits to represent the sign, and use the remaining 31 bits to store the magnitude of the integer, which may then range from 0 to $2^{31} - 1$. However, nearly all machines use a more clever representation called 2's *complement*.[5] A nonnegative integer x, where $0 \leq x \leq 2^{31} - 1$, is stored as the binary representation of x, but a negative integer $-y$, where $1 \leq y \leq 2^{31}$, is stored as the binary representation of the positive integer

$$2^{32} - y. \qquad (3.1)$$

For example, the integer -71 is stored as

$$\boxed{11111111111111111111111110111001}.$$

In order to see that this is correct, let us add the 2's complement representations for 71 and -71 together:

$$\begin{aligned}
&(\ 00000000000000000000000001000111\ )_2 \\
+\ &(\ 11111111111111111111111110111001\ )_2 \\
=\ &(\ 100000000000000000000000000000000\ )_2.
\end{aligned}$$

---

[5]There is a third system called 1's complement, where a negative integer $-y$ is stored as the binary representation of $2^{32} - y - 1$. This system was used by some supercomputers in the 1960s and 1970s but is now obsolete.

Adding in binary by hand is like adding in decimal. Proceed bitwise right to left; when 1 and 1 are added together, the result is 10 (base 2), so the resulting bit is set to 0 and the 1 is carried over to the next bit to the left. The sum of the representations for 71 and for -71 is thus the bitstring for 2^{32}, as required by the definition (3.1). The bit in the leftmost position of the sum cannot be stored in the 32-bit word and is called an *overflow bit*. If it is discarded, the result is 0—exactly what we want for the result of $71 + (-71)$. This is the motivation for the 2's complement representation.

Exercise 3.1 *Using a 32-bit word, how many different integers can be represented by (a) sign and modulus; (b) 2's complement? Express the answer using powers of 2. For which of these two systems is the representation for zero unique?*

Exercise 3.2 *Suppose we wish to store integers using only a 16-bit half-word (2 bytes). This is called a* short integer *format. What is the range of integers that can be stored using 2's complement? Express the answer using powers of 2 and also translate the numbers into decimal notation.*

Exercise 3.3 *Using an 8-bit format for simplicity, give the 2's complement representation for the following integers: 1, 10, 100, -1, -10, and -100. Verify that addition of a negative number to its positive counterpart yields zero, as required, when the overflow bit is discarded.*

Exercise 3.4 *Show that if an integer x between -2^{31} and $2^{31} - 1$ is represented using 2's complement in a 32-bit word, the leftmost bit is 1 if x is negative and 0 if x is positive or 0.*

Exercise 3.5 *An easy way to convert the representation of a nonnegative integer x to the 2's complement representation for $-x$ begins by changing all 0 bits to 1s and all 1 bits to 0s. One more step is necessary to complete the process; what is it, and why?*

All computers provide hardware instructions for adding integers. If two positive integers are added together, the result may give an integer greater than or equal to 2^{31}. In this case, we say that *integer overflow* occurs. One would hope that this leads to an informative error message for the user, but whether or not this happens depends on the programming language and compiler being used. In some cases, the overflow bits may be discarded and the programmer must be alert to prevent this from happening.[6] The same problem may occur if two negative integers are added together, giving a negative integer with magnitude greater than 2^{31}.

On the other hand, if two integers with opposite sign are added together, integer overflow cannot occur, although an overflow bit may arise when the 2's complement bitstrings are added together. Consider the operation

$$x + (-y),$$

where

$$0 \leq x \leq 2^{31} - 1 \quad \text{and} \quad 1 \leq y \leq 2^{31}.$$

Clearly, it is possible to store the desired result $x - y$ without integer overflow. The result may be positive, negative, or zero, depending on whether $x > y$, $x = y$, or $x < y$. Now let us see what happens if we add the 2's complement representations for

---

[6]The IEEE floating point standard, to be introduced in the next chapter, says nothing about requirements for integer arithmetic.

x and $-y$, i.e., the bitstrings for the nonnegative numbers x and $2^{32} - y$. We obtain the bitstring for
$$2^{32} + x - y = 2^{32} - (y - x).$$
If $x \geq y$, the leftmost bit of the result is an overflow bit, corresponding to the power 2^{32}, but this bit can be discarded, giving the correct result $x - y$. If $x < y$, the result fits in 32 bits with no overflow bit, and we have the desired result, since it represents the negative value $-(y - x)$ in 2's complement.

This demonstrates an important property of 2's complement representation: no special hardware is needed for integer subtraction. The addition hardware can be used once the negative number $-y$ has been represented using 2's complement.

Exercise 3.6 *Show the details for the integer sums* $50 + (-100)$, $100 + (-50)$, *and* $50 + 50$, *using an 8-bit format.*

Besides addition, the other standard hardware operations on integer operands are multiplication and division, where by the latter, we mean integer division, yielding an integer quotient. Multiplication may give integer overflow. Integer division by zero normally leads to program termination and an error message for the user

Exercise 3.7 *(D. Goldberg) Besides division by zero, is there any other division operation that could result in integer overflow?*

Fixed Point

Now let us turn to the representation of nonintegral real numbers. Rational numbers could be represented by pairs of integers, the numerator and denominator. This has the advantage of accuracy but the disadvantage of being very inconvenient for arithmetic. Systems that represent rational numbers in this way are said to be *symbolic* rather than numeric. However, for most numerical computing purposes, real numbers, whether rational or irrational, are approximately stored using the binary representation of the number. There are two possible methods, called fixed point and floating point.

In *fixed point* representation, the computer word may be viewed as divided into three fields: one 1-bit field for the sign of the number, one field of bits for the binary representation of the number before the binary point, and one field of bits for the binary representation after the binary point. For example, in a 32-bit word with field widths of 15 and 16, respectively, the number $11/2$ (see (2.2)) would be stored as

| 0 | 000000000000101 | 1000000000000000 |,

while the number $1/10$ would be approximately stored as

| 0 | 000000000000000 | 0001100110011001 |.

The fixed point system is severely limited by the size of the numbers it can store. In the example just given, only numbers ranging in size from (exactly) 2^{-16} to (slightly less than) 2^{15} could be stored. This is not adequate for many applications. Therefore, fixed point representation is rarely used for numerical computing.

Floating Point

Floating point representation is based on *exponential* (or *scientific*) notation. In exponential notation, a nonzero real number x is expressed in decimal as
$$x = \pm S \times 10^E, \quad \text{where } 1 \leq S < 10,$$

and E is an integer. The numbers S and E are called the *significand*[7] and the *exponent*, respectively. For example, the exponential representation of 365.25 is 3.6525×10^2, and the exponential representation of 0.00036525 is 3.6525×10^{-4}. It is always possible to satisfy the requirement that $1 \leq S < 10$, as S can be obtained from x by repeatedly multiplying or dividing by 10, decrementing or incrementing the exponent E accordingly. We can imagine that the *decimal point floats* to the position immediately after the first nonzero digit in the decimal expansion of the number—hence the name floating point.

For representation on the computer, we prefer base 2 to base 10, so we write a nonzero number x in the form

$$x = \pm S \times 2^E, \quad \text{where } 1 \leq S < 2. \tag{3.2}$$

Consequently, the binary expansion of the significand is

$$S = (b_0.b_1b_2b_3\ldots)_2 \quad \text{with} \quad b_0 = 1. \tag{3.3}$$

For example, the number 11/2 is expressed as

$$\frac{11}{2} = (1.011)_2 \times 2^2.$$

Now it is the *binary point* that *floats* to the position after the first nonzero bit in the binary expansion of x, changing the exponent E accordingly. Of course, this is not possible if the number x is zero, but at present we are considering only the nonzero case. Since b_0 is 1, we may write

$$S = (1.b_1b_2b_3\ldots)_2.$$

The bits following the binary point are called the *fractional* part of the significand. We say that (3.2), (3.3) is the *normalized* representation of x, and the process of obtaining it is called *normalization*.

To store normalized numbers, we divide the computer word into three fields to represent the sign, the exponent E, and the significand S, respectively. A 32-bit word could be divided into fields as follows: 1 bit for the sign, 8 bits for the exponent, and 23 bits for the significand. The sign bit is 0 for positive numbers and 1 for negative numbers. Since the exponent field is 8 bits, it can be used to represent exponents E between -128 and 127 (for example, using 2's complement, though this is not the way it is normally done). The 23 significand bits can be used to store the first 23 bits after the binary point in the binary expansion of S, namely, $b_1, \ldots, b_{23}$. It is not necessary to store b_0, since we know it has the value 1: we say that b_0 is a *hidden bit*. Of course, it might not be possible to store the number x with such a scheme, either because E is outside the permissible range -128 to 127 or because the bits $b_{24}, b_{25}, \ldots$ in the binary expansion of S are not all zero. A real number is called a *floating point number* if it can be stored *exactly* on the computer using the given floating point representation scheme. If a number x is not a floating point number, it must be *rounded* before it can be stored on the computer. This will be discussed later.

Using this idea, the number 11/2 would be stored as

| 0 | ebits(2) | 01100000000000000000000 |

and the number

$$71 = (1.000111)_2 \times 2^6$$

---

[7] Also known as the *mantissa*.

would be stored as

| 0 | ebits(6) | 00011100000000000000000 |

To avoid confusion, the bits in the exponent field are not shown explicitly, for the moment, but written in the functional form "ebits(E)". Since the bitstring stored in the significand field is actually the *fractional part* of the significand, we also refer to this field as the *fraction field*. Given a string of bits in the fraction field, it is necessary to imagine that the symbols "1." appear in front of the string, even though these symbols are not stored.

In this scheme, if x is exactly a power of 2, so that the significand is the number 1.0, the bits stored in the fraction field are all 0 (since b_0 is not stored). For example,

$$1 = (1.000\ldots)_2 \times 2^0$$

would be stored as

| 0 | ebits(0) | 00000000000000000000000 |

and the number

$$1024 = (1.000\ldots)_2 \times 2^{10}$$

would be stored as

| 0 | ebits(10) | 00000000000000000000000 |

Now consider the much larger number

$$2^{71} = (1.000\ldots)_2 \times 2^{71}.$$

This integer is much too large to store in a 32-bit word using the integer format discussed earlier. However, there is no difficulty representing it in floating point, using the representation

| 0 | ebits(71) | 00000000000000000000000 |

Exercise 3.8 *What is the largest floating point number in this system, assuming the significand field can store only the bits $b_1 \ldots b_{23}$ and the exponent is limited by $-128 \leq E \leq 127$? Don't forget that the hidden bit, b_0, is 1.*

Exercise 3.9 *What is the smallest positive floating point number in this system? Remember the requirement that the number is normalized, i.e., that the hidden bit, b_0, is 1.*

Exercise 3.10 *What is the smallest positive integer that is not exactly representable as a floating point number in this system?*

Exercise 3.11 *Suppose we change (3.2) so that the bounds on the significand are $\frac{1}{2} \leq S < 1$, change (3.3) to*

$$S = (0.b_1 b_2 b_3 b_4 \ldots)_2, \quad \text{with} \quad b_1 = 1,$$

and change our floating point system so that the significand field stores only the bits $b_2, \ldots, b_{24}$, with the exponent limited by $-128 \leq E \leq 127$ as before. What is the largest floating point number in this system? What is the smallest positive floating point number in this system (remembering that the number must be normalized with the hidden bit $b_1 = 1$)? What is the smallest positive integer that is not exactly representable as a floating point number in this system?

If a number x does not have a finite binary expansion, we must terminate its expansion somewhere. For example, consider the number

$$1/10 = (0.0001100110011\ldots)_2.$$

If we truncate this to 23 bits after the binary point, we obtain

$$(0.00011001100110011001100)_2.$$

However, if we then normalize this to obtain

$$(1.1001100110011001100)_2 \times 2^{-4},$$

so that there is a 1 before the binary point, we find that we now have only 19 correct bits after the binary point. This leads to the unnecessarily inaccurate representation

| 0 | ebits(−4) | 10011001100110011000000 |

having 4 incorrect bits at the end of the significand. Clearly, this is not a good idea. It is preferable to *first* normalize and *then* truncate, so that we retain 23 correct bits after the binary point:

| 0 | ebits(−4) | 10011001100110011001100 |

This way all the available bits are used. The alert reader will note that it might be better to round the final bit up to 1. We will discuss this later.

Precision, Machine Epsilon, and Ulp

The *precision* of the floating point system is the number of bits in the significand (including the hidden bit). We denote the precision by p. In the system just described, $p = 24$ (23 stored bits in the fractional part of the significand and 1 leading hidden bit). Any normalized floating point number with precision p can be expressed as

$$x = \pm(1.b_1 b_2 \ldots b_{p-2} b_{p-1})_2 \times 2^E. \quad (3.4)$$

The smallest such x that is greater than 1 is

$$(1.00\ldots01)_2 = 1 + 2^{-(p-1)}.$$

We give a special name, *machine epsilon*,[8] to the gap between this number and the number 1, and we write this as

$$\epsilon = (0.00\ldots01)_2 = 2^{-(p-1)}. \quad (3.5)$$

More generally, for a floating point number x given by (3.4) we define

$$\text{ulp}(x) = (0.00\ldots01)_2 \times 2^E = 2^{-(p-1)} \times 2^E = \epsilon \times 2^E. \quad (3.6)$$

Ulp is short for *unit in the last place*. If $x > 0$, then ulp(x) is the gap between x and the next larger floating point number. If $x < 0$, ulp(x) is the gap between x and the next smaller floating point number (larger in absolute value).

Exercise 3.12 *Let the precision $p = 24$, so $\epsilon = 2^{-23}$. Determine* ulp(x) *for x having the following values: 0.25, 2, 3, 4, 10, 100, 1030. Give your answer as a power of 2; do not convert this to decimal.*

---

[8] Many authors define machine epsilon to be half the gap. We follow [Hig96] in our definitions of ϵ and ulp.

The Special Number Zero

So far, we have discussed only nonzero numbers. The number *zero* is special. It cannot be normalized, since all the bits in its representation are zero. Thus, it cannot be represented using the scheme described so far. A pattern of all zeros in the significand represents the significand 1.0, not 0.0, since the bit b_0 is hidden. There are two ways to address this difficulty. The first, which was used by most floating point implementations until about 1975, is to give up the idea of a hidden bit and instead insist that the leading bit b_0 in the binary representation of a nonzero number must be stored explicitly, even though it is always 1. In this way, the number zero can be represented by a significand that has all zero bits. This approach effectively reduces the precision of the system by one bit, because, to make room for b_0, we must give up storing the final bit (b_{23} in the system described above). The second approach is to use a special string in the exponent field to signal that the number is zero. This reduces by one the number of possible exponents E that are allowed for representing nonzero numbers. This is the approach taken by the IEEE standard, to be discussed in the next chapter. In either case, there is the question of what to do about the sign of zero. Traditionally, this was ignored, but we shall see a different approach in the next chapter.

The Toy Number System

It is quite instructive to suppose that the computer word size is much smaller than 32 bits and work out in detail what all the possible floating point numbers are in such a case. Suppose that all numbers have the form

$$\pm(b_0.b_1b_2)_2 \times 2^E,$$

with b_0 stored explicitly and all nonzero numbers required to be normalized. Thus, b_0 is allowed to be zero only if b_1 and b_2 are also zero, indicating that the number represented is zero. Suppose also that the only possible values for the exponent E are -1, 0, and 1. We shall call this system the *toy floating point number system*. The set of toy floating point numbers is shown in Figure 3.1.

Figure 3.1: The Toy Floating Point Numbers

The precision of the toy system is $p = 3$. The largest number is $(1\ 11)_2 \times 2^1 = (3.5)_{10}$, and the smallest positive number is $(1.00)_2 \times 2^{-1} = (0.5)_{10}$. Since the next floating point number bigger than 1 is 1.25, machine epsilon for the toy system is $\epsilon = 0.25$. Note that the gap between floating point numbers becomes *smaller* as the magnitudes of the numbers themselves get smaller, and *bigger* as the numbers get bigger. Specifically, consider the positive floating point numbers with $E = 0$: these are the numbers 1, 1.25, 1.5, and 1.75. For each of these numbers, say x, the gap between x and the next floating point number larger than x, i.e., ulp(x), is machine epsilon, $\epsilon = 0.25$. For the positive floating point numbers x with $E = 1$, the gap is twice as big, i.e., $\mathrm{ulp}(x) = 2\epsilon$, and for those x with $E = -1$, the gap is $\mathrm{ulp}(x) = \frac{1}{2}\epsilon$. Summarizing, the gap between a positive toy floating point number $x = (b_0.b_1b_2)_2 \times 2^E$ and the next bigger toy floating point number is

$$\mathrm{ulp}(x) = \epsilon \times 2^E,$$

as already noted in (3.6).

Another important observation to make about Figure 3.1 is that the gaps between zero and ± 0.5 are much greater than the gaps between numbers ranging from ± 0.5 to ± 1. We shall show in the next chapter how these gaps can be filled in with the introduction of *subnormal* numbers.

Exercise 3.13 *Suppose we add another bit to the toy number system, allowing significands of the form $b_0.b_1b_2b_3$, with b_0 stored explicitly as before and all nonzero numbers required to be normalized. The restrictions on the exponent are unchanged. Mark the new numbers on a copy of Figure* 3.1.

Fixed Point versus Floating Point

Some of the early computers used fixed point representation and some used floating point. Von Neumann was initially skeptical of floating point and promoted the use of fixed point representation. He was well aware that the range limitations of fixed point would be too severe to be practical, but he believed that the necessary scaling by a power of 2 should be done by the programmer, not the machine; he argued that bits were too precious to be wasted on storing an exponent when they could be used to extend the precision of the significand. Wilkinson experimented extensively with a compromise system called block floating point, where an automatic scale factor is maintained for a vector, i.e., for a block of many numbers, instead of one scale factor per number. This means that only the largest number (in absolute value) in the vector is sure to be normalized; if a vector contains numbers with widely varying magnitudes, those with smaller magnitudes are stored much less accurately. By the late 1950s it was apparent that the floating point system is far more versatile and efficient than fixed point or block floating point.

Knuth [Knu98, pp. 196, 225] attributes the origins of floating point notation to the Babylonians. In their base 60 number system, zero was never used at the end of a number, and hence a power of 60 was always implicit. The Babylonians, like von Neumann, did not explicitly store their exponents.

Chapter 4
IEEE Floating Point Representation

Floating point computation was in standard use by the mid 1950s. During the subsequent two decades, each computer manufacturer developed its own floating point system, leading to much inconsistency in how one program might behave on different machines. For example, although most machines developed during this period used binary floating point systems roughly similar to the one described in the previous chapter, the IBM 360/370 series, which dominated computing during the 1960s and 1970s, used a hexadecimal system (base 16). On these machines, the significand is stored using 24 bits, to be interpreted as 6 hexadecimal digits, leaving 1 bit for the sign and 7 bits for the exponent (representing a power of 16). Normalization requires only that the first hexadecimal digit be nonzero; consequently, the significand could have up to 3 leading zero bits. Therefore, the accuracy of the significands ranges from 21 to 24 bits; some numbers (such as 1/10; see (2.3)) are represented less accurately than on a binary machine. One motivation for this design was to reduce the bit shifting required during floating point add and subtract operations. Another benefit is that the hexadecimal base allows a much greater range of normalized floating point numbers than a binary system permits.

In addition to inconsistencies of representation, there were also many inconsistencies in the properties of floating point arithmetic. See Chapter 6 for examples of difficulties that could arise unexpectedly on some machines. Consequently, it was very difficult to write *portable software* that would work properly on all machines. Programmers needed to be aware of various difficulties that might arise on different machines and attempt to forestall them.

A Historic Collaboration: IEEE p754

In an extraordinary cooperation between academic computer scientists and microprocessor chip designers, a standard for binary floating point representation and arithmetic was developed in the late 1970s and early 1980s and, most importantly, was followed carefully by the microprocessor industry. As this was the beginning of the personal computer revolution, the impact was enormous. The group of scientists who wrote the standard did so under the auspices of the Institute for Electrical and Electronics Engineers;[8] the group was known as IEEE p754. The academic computer scientists on the committee were led by William Kahan of the University of

---
[8] Abbreviated IEEE, pronounced "I triple E."

California at Berkeley; industrial participants included representatives from Apple, Digital Equipment Corporation (DEC), Intel, Hewlett-Packard, Motorola, and National Semiconductor. Kahan's interest in the project had been sparked originally by the efforts of John Palmer, of Intel, to ensure that Intel's new 8087 chip would have the best possible floating point arithmetic. An early document that included many of the ideas adopted by the standard was written in 1979 by Kahan, Coonen, and Stone; see [Cod81]. Kahan was awarded the 1989 Turing Prize by the Association of Computing Machinery for his work in leading IEEE p754.

In [Sev98], Kahan recalled: "It was remarkable that so many hardware people there, knowing how difficult p754 would be, agreed that it should benefit the community at large. If it encouraged the production of floating-point software and eased the development of reliable software, it would help create a larger market for everyone's hardware. This degree of altruism was so astonishing that MATLAB's creator Cleve Moler used to advise foreign visitors not to miss the country's two most awesome spectacles: the Grand Canyon, and meetings of IEEE p754."

The IEEE standard for binary floating point arithmetic was published in 1985, when it became known officially as ANSI/IEEE Std 754-1985 [IEE85]. In 1989, it received international endorsement as IEC 559, later designated IEC 60559. A second IEEE floating point standard, for radix-independent floating point arithmetic, ANSI/IEEE Std 854-1987 [IEE87], was adopted in 1987. The second standard was motivated by the existence of decimal, rather than binary, floating point machines, particularly hand-held calculators, and set requirements for both binary and decimal floating point arithmetic in a common framework. The demands for binary arithmetic imposed by IEEE 854 are consistent with those previously established by IEEE 754. In this book, when we write "the IEEE standard," we refer to the binary standard, IEEE 754. The term "IEEE arithmetic" is used to mean floating point arithmetic that is in compliance with the IEEE standard. For more on the development of the standard, see [Cod81] and [PH97, Section 4.12]. At the time of this writing, the standard is being considered for revision [IEE-R].

IEEE Floating Point Essentials

The IEEE standard has three very important requirements:

- consistent representation of floating point numbers by all machines adopting the standard (discussed in this chapter);

- correctly rounded floating point operations, using various rounding modes (see Chapters 5 and 6);

- consistent treatment of exceptional situations such as division by zero (see Chapter 7).

In the basic IEEE formats, the leading bit of a normalized number is hidden, as described in the previous chapter. Thus, a special representation is needed for storing zero. However, zero is not the only number for which the IEEE standard has a special representation. Another special number, not used on older machines, is the number ∞. This allows the possibility of dividing a positive number by zero and storing a sensible mathematical result, namely ∞, instead of terminating with an overflow message. This turns out to be very useful, as we shall see later, although one must be careful about what is meant by such a result. One question that immediately arises is: what about $-\infty$? It turns out to be convenient to have representations for $-\infty$ as well as ∞, and for -0 as well as 0. We will give more details in Chapter 7, but note for

Table 4.1: IEEE Single Format

| ± | $a_1 a_2 a_3 \ldots a_8$ | $b_1 b_2 b_3 \ldots b_{23}$ |

If exponent bitstring $a_1 \ldots a_8$ is	Then numerical value represented is
$(00000000)_2 = (0)_{10}$	$\pm (0.b_1 b_2 b_3 \ldots b_{23})_2 \times 2^{-126}$
$(00000001)_2 = (1)_{10}$	$\pm (1.b_1 b_2 b_3 \ldots b_{23})_2 \times 2^{-126}$
$(00000010)_2 = (2)_{10}$	$\pm (1.b_1 b_2 b_3 \ldots b_{23})_2 \times 2^{-125}$
$(00000011)_2 = (3)_{10}$	$\pm (1.b_1 b_2 b_3 \ldots b_{23})_2 \times 2^{-124}$
↓	↓
$(01111111)_2 = (127)_{10}$	$\pm (1.b_1 b_2 b_3 \ldots b_{23})_2 \times 2^0$
$(10000000)_2 = (128)_{10}$	$\pm (1.b_1 b_2 b_3 \ldots b_{23})_2 \times 2^1$
↓	↓
$(11111100)_2 = (252)_{10}$	$\pm (1.b_1 b_2 b_3 \ldots b_{23})_2 \times 2^{125}$
$(11111101)_2 = (253)_{10}$	$\pm (1.b_1 b_2 b_3 \ldots b_{23})_2 \times 2^{126}$
$(11111110)_2 = (254)_{10}$	$\pm (1.b_1 b_2 b_3 \ldots b_{23})_2 \times 2^{127}$
$(11111111)_2 = (255)_{10}$	$\pm\infty$ if $b_1 = \cdots = b_{23} = 0$, NaN otherwise

now that -0 and 0 are *two different representations for the same number* zero, while $-\infty$ and ∞ represent *two very different numbers*. Another special number is NaN, which stands for "Not a Number" and is accordingly not a number at all, but an error pattern. This too will be discussed later. All of these special numbers, as well as others called subnormal numbers, are represented through the use of a specific bit pattern in the exponent field.

The Single Format

The IEEE standard specifies two basic representation formats, *single* and *double*. *Single format* numbers use a 32-bit word and their representations are summarized in Table 4.1.

Let us discuss Table 4.1 in some detail. The ± refers to the sign of the number, a zero bit being used to represent a positive sign. The first line shows that the representation for zero requires a special zero bitstring for the exponent field *as well as* a zero bitstring for the fraction field, i.e.,

| ± | 00000000 | 00000000000000000000000 |

No other line in the table can be used to represent the number zero, for all lines except the first and the last represent normalized numbers, with an initial bit equal to 1; this is the one that is hidden. In the case of the first line of the table, the hidden bit is 0, not 1. The 2^{-126} in the first line is confusing at first sight, but let us ignore that for the moment since $(0.000\ldots 0)_2 \times 2^{-126}$ is certainly one way to write the number 0. In the case when the exponent field has a zero bitstring but the fraction field has a nonzero bitstring, the number represented is said to be *subnormal*.[9] Let us postpone the discussion of subnormal numbers for the moment and go on to the other lines of the table.

All the lines of Table 4.1 except the first and the last refer to the normalized numbers, i.e., all the floating point numbers that are not special in some way. Note

---

[9] The word *denormalized* was used in IEEE 754. The word *subnormal* replaced it in IEEE 854.

especially the relationship between the exponent bitstring $a_1 a_2 a_3 \ldots a_8$ and the actual exponent E. We see that the exponent representation does not use either the sign-and-modulus or the 2's complement integer representation discussed in the previous chapter, but something called *biased representation*; the bitstring that is stored is the binary representation of $E + 127$. The number 127, which is added to the desired exponent E, is called the *exponent bias*. For example, the number $1 = (1.000\ldots 0)_2 \times 2^0$ is stored as

| 0 | 01111111 | 00000000000000000000000 |

Here the exponent bitstring is the binary representation for $0 + 127$ and the fraction bitstring is the binary representation for 0 (the fractional part of 1.0). The number $11/2 = (1.011)_2 \times 2^2$ is stored as

| 0 | 10000001 | 01100000000000000000000 |

The number $1/10 = (1.100110011\ldots)_2 \times 2^{-4}$ has a nonterminating binary expansion. If we truncate this to fit the significand field size, we find that $1/10$ is stored as

| 0 | 01111011 | 10011001100110011001100 |

We shall see other rounding options in the next chapter.

The range of exponent field bitstrings for normalized numbers is 00000001 to 11111110 (the decimal numbers 1 through 254), representing actual exponents from $E_{\min} = -126$ to $E_{\max} = 127$. The smallest positive normalized number that can be stored is represented by

| 0 | 00000001 | 00000000000000000000000 |

and we denote this by

$$N_{\min} = (1.000\ldots 0)_2 \times 2^{-126} = 2^{-126} \approx 1.2 \times 10^{-38}. \tag{4.1}$$

The largest normalized number (equivalently, the largest finite number) is represented by

| 0 | 11111110 | 11111111111111111111111 |

and we denote this by

$$N_{\max} = (1.111\ldots 1)_2 \times 2^{127} = (2 - 2^{-23}) \times 2^{127} \approx 2^{128} \approx 3.4 \times 10^{38}. \tag{4.2}$$

The last line of Table 4.1 shows that an exponent bitstring consisting of all 1s is a special pattern used to represent $\pm\infty$ or NaN, depending on the fraction bitstring. We will discuss these in Chapter 7.

Subnormals

Finally, let us return to the first line of the table. The idea here is as follows: although 2^{-126} is the smallest normalized number that can be represented, we can use the combination of the special zero exponent bitstring and a nonzero fraction bitstring to represent smaller numbers called subnormal numbers. For example, 2^{-127}, which is the same as $(0.1)_2 \times 2^{-126}$, is represented as

| 0 | 00000000 | 10000000000000000000000 |

while $2^{-149} = (0.0000\ldots 01)_2 \times 2^{-126}$ (with 22 zero bits after the binary point) is stored as

| 0 | 00000000 | 00000000000000000000001 |

Figure 4.1: The Toy System Including Subnormal Numbers

This is the smallest positive number that can be stored. Now we see the reason for the 2^{-126} in the first line. It allows us to represent numbers in the range immediately below the smallest positive normalized number. Subnormal numbers cannot be normalized, since normalization would result in an exponent that does not fit in the field.

Let us return to our example of the toy system with a tiny word size, illustrated in Figure 3.1, and see how the addition of subnormal numbers changes it. We get six extra numbers: $\pm(0.11)_2 \times 2^{-1} = 3/8$, $\pm(0.10)_2 \times 2^{-1} = 1/4$, and $\pm(0.01)_2 \times 2^{-1} = 1/8$; these are shown in Figure 4.1. Note that *the gaps between zero and ± 0.5 are evenly filled in by the subnormal numbers*, using the same spacing as that between the numbers in the range ± 0.5 to ± 1.

Subnormal numbers are have less room for nonzero bits in the fraction field than normalized numbers. Consequently, the accuracy to which they can approximate a number drops as the size of the subnormal number decreases. Thus $(1/10) \times 2^{-123} = (0.11001100\ldots)_2 \times 2^{-126}$ is truncated to

| 0 | 00000000 | 11001100110011001100110 |

while $(1/10) \times 2^{-135} = (0.11001100\ldots)_2 \times 2^{-138}$ is truncated to

| 0 | 00000000 | 00000000000011001100110 |

Exercise 4.1 *Determine the IEEE single format floating point representation for the following numbers: 2, 30, 31, 32, 33, 23/4, $(23/4) \times 2^{100}$, $(23/4) \times 2^{-100}$, and $(23/4) \times 2^{-135}$. Truncating the significand as in the 1/10 example, do the same for the numbers $1/5 = (1/10) \times 2$, $1024/5 = (1/10) \times 2^{11}$, and $(1/10) \times 2^{-140}$, using (2.3) to avoid decimal-to-binary conversions.*

Exercise 4.2 *What is the gap between 2 and the first IEEE single format number larger than 2? What is the gap between 1024 and the first IEEE single format number larger than 1024?*

Exercise 4.3 *Give an algorithm that, given two IEEE single format floating point numbers x and y, determines whether x is less than, equal to, or greater than y, by comparing their representations bitwise from left to right, stopping as soon as the first differing bit is encountered. Assume that neither x nor y is ± 0, $\pm \infty$, or NaN. The fact that such a comparison can be done easily motivates biased exponent representation. It also justifies referring to the left end of the representation as the "most significant" end.*

Exercise 4.4 *This extends Exercise 3.13, which considered the toy number system with one additional bit in the significand. Mark the subnormal numbers in this system on the modified copy of Figure 3.1 that you used to answer Exercise 3.13.*

Table 4.2: IEEE Double Format

| $\pm$ | $a_1 a_2 a_3 \ldots a_{11}$ | $b_1 b_2 b_3 \ldots b_{52}$ |

If exponent bitstring is $a_1 \ldots a_{11}$	Then numerical value represented is
$(00000000000)_2 = (0)_{10}$	$\pm(0.b_1 b_2 b_3 \ldots b_{52})_2 \times 2^{-1022}$
$(00000000001)_2 = (1)_{10}$	$\pm(1.b_1 b_2 b_3 \ldots b_{52})_2 \times 2^{-1022}$
$(00000000010)_2 = (2)_{10}$	$\pm(1.b_1 b_2 b_3 \ldots b_{52})_2 \times 2^{-1021}$
$(00000000011)_2 = (3)_{10}$	$\pm(1.b_1 b_2 b_3 \ldots b_{52})_2 \times 2^{-1020}$
$\downarrow$	$\downarrow$
$(01111111111)_2 = (1023)_{10}$	$\pm(1.b_1 b_2 b_3 \ldots b_{52})_2 \times 2^0$
$(10000000000)_2 = (1024)_{10}$	$\pm(1.b_1 b_2 b_3 \ldots b_{52})_2 \times 2^1$
$\downarrow$	$\downarrow$
$(11111111100)_2 = (2044)_{10}$	$\pm(1.b_1 b_2 b_3 \ldots b_{52})_2 \times 2^{1021}$
$(11111111101)_2 = (2045)_{10}$	$\pm(1.b_1 b_2 b_3 \ldots b_{52})_2 \times 2^{1022}$
$(11111111110)_2 = (2046)_{10}$	$\pm(1.b_1 b_2 b_3 \ldots b_{52})_2 \times 2^{1023}$
$(11111111111)_2 = (2047)_{10}$	$\pm\infty$ if $b_1 = \cdots = b_{52} = 0$, NaN otherwise

Table 4.3: Range of IEEE Floating Point Formats

Format	$E_{\min}$	$E_{\max}$	$N_{\min}$	$N_{\max}$
Single	-126	127	$2^{-126} \approx 1.2 \times 10^{-38}$	$\approx 2^{128} \approx 3.4 \times 10^{38}$
Double	-1022	1023	$2^{-1022} \approx 2.2 \times 10^{-308}$	$\approx 2^{1024} \approx 1.8 \times 10^{308}$

The Double Format

The single format is not adequate for many applications, either because higher precision is desired or (less often) because a greater exponent range is needed. The IEEE standard specifies a second basic format, *double*, which uses a 64-bit double word. Details are shown in Table 4.2. The ideas are the same as before; only the field widths and exponent bias are different. Now the exponents range from $E_{\min} = -1022$ to $E_{\max} = 1023$, and the number of bits in the fraction field is 52. Numbers with no finite binary expansion, such as $1/10$ or π, are represented more accurately with the double format than they are with the single format. The smallest positive normalized double format number is

$$N_{\min} = 2^{-1022} \approx 2.2 \times 10^{-308} \tag{4.3}$$

and the largest is

$$N_{\max} = (2 - 2^{-52}) \times 2^{1023} \approx 1.8 \times 10^{308}. \tag{4.4}$$

We summarize the bounds on the exponents and the values of the smallest and largest normalized numbers given in (4.1), (4.2), (4.3), and (4.4) in Table 4.3.

Single versus Double

The IEEE standard requires that machines provide the single format. The double format is optional, but is provided by almost all computers that implement the standard,

CHAPTER 4. IEEE FLOATING POINT REPRESENTATION

Table 4.4: Precision of IEEE Floating Point Formats

Format	Precision	Machine Epsilon
Single	$p = 24$	$\epsilon = 2^{-23} \approx 1.2 \times 10^{-7}$
Double	$p = 53$	$\epsilon = 2^{-52} \approx 2.2 \times 10^{-16}$
Extended (Intel)	$p = 64$	$\epsilon = 2^{-63} \approx 1.1 \times 10^{-19}$

and we shall therefore *assume that the double format is always provided*. Support for the requirements may be provided by hardware or software, but almost all machines have hardware support for both the single and double formats. Because of its greater precision, the double format is preferred for most applications in scientific computing, though the single format provides an efficient way to store huge quantities of data.

The Extended Format

The standard also strongly recommends support for an extended format, with at least 15 bits available for the exponent and at least 63 bits for the fractional part of the significand. The Intel microprocessors implement arithmetic with the extended format in hardware, using 80-bit registers, with 1 bit for the sign, 15 bits for the exponent, and 64 bits for the significand. The leading bit of a normalized or subnormal number is not hidden as it is in the single and double formats, but is explicitly stored Otherwise, the format is much the same as single and double. Other machines, such as the Sparc microprocessor used in Sun workstations, implement extended precision arithmetic in software using 128 bits. Consequently, computations with the extended format are fast on an Intel microprocessor but relatively slow on a Sparc.

Precision and Machine Epsilon of the IEEE Formats

Recall from the previous chapter that we use the notation p (precision) to denote the number of bits in the significand and ϵ (machine epsilon) to mean the gap between 1 and the next larger floating point number. The precision of the IEEE single format is $p = 24$ (including the hidden bit); for the double format it is $p = 53$ (again, including the hidden bit). When we speak of *single precision*, we mean the precision of the IEEE single format ($p = 24$); likewise *double precision* means the precision of the IEEE double format ($p = 53$).[10] The precision of the Intel extended format is $p = 64$, since it has no hidden bit. The first single format number larger than 1 is $1 + 2^{-23}$, and the first double format number larger than 1 is $1 + 2^{-52}$. With the Intel extended format, since there is no hidden bit, $1 + 2^{-64}$ cannot be stored exactly; the first extended format number larger than 1 is $1 + 2^{-63}$. These observations are summarized in Table 4.4, showing the values of the precision p and machine epsilon ϵ, together with its approximate decimal equivalent, for each of the single, double, and Intel extended formats.

Significant Digits

The single precision $p = 24$ corresponds to *approximately* 7 *significant decimal digits*, since
$$2^{-24} \approx 10^{-7}.$$

---

[10]Often the terms *single precision* and *double precision* are also used to mean the single format and double format, respectively.

Here $\approx$ means *approximately equals*.[11] Equivalently,

$$\log_{10}(2^{24}) \approx 7. \tag{4.5}$$

The double precision $p = 53$ corresponds to *approximately* 16 *significant decimal digits*, and the Intel extended precision $p = 64$ corresponds to *approximately* 19 *significant decimal digits*. We deliberately use the word *approximately* here, because defining *significant digits* is problematic. The IEEE single representation for

$$\pi = 3.141592653\ldots$$

is, when converted to decimal,

$$3.141592741\ldots.$$

To how many digits does this approximate π? We might say 7, since the first 7 digits of both numbers are the same, or we might say 8, since if we round both numbers to 8 digits, rounding π up and the approximation down, we get the same number 3.1415927. See [Hig96] for a discussion of the difficulties involved in using definitions like these to define "significant digits." We will see a better way to measure accurate digits in the next chapter.

Big and Little Endian

Modern computers address memory by bytes. A 32-bit word consists of 4 consecutive bytes with addresses, say, $B_1, \ldots, B_4$, where $B_4 = B_1 + 3$. Suppose we store a single format floating point number in this word. We know from Table 4.1 that a single format number has the bit format

$$\sigma a_1 a_2 a_3 \ldots a_8 b_1 b_2 b_3 \ldots b_{23},$$

where σ is the sign bit. This corresponds to 4 bytes, of which the "most significant" (see Exercise 4.3) is the byte

$$\sigma a_1 a_2 a_3 a_4 a_5 a_6 a_7.$$

Let us ask the question: is this most significant byte stored in byte B_1 or byte B_4? Surprisingly, it turns out that the answer depends on the machine. Addressing systems for which the answer is B_1 are called *Big Endian* (the first byte B_1 stores the "big end" of the floating point word). Addressing systems for which the answer is B_4 are called *Little Endian* (the first byte B_1 stores the "little end," i.e., the least significant byte, of the floating point word). Sun and IBM machines use Big Endian addressing, while Intel uses Little Endian addressing. Some microprocessors, such as the DEC Alpha, can operate in either mode. The fact that different machines use different schemes means that care must be taken when passing data from one machine to another. The addressing schemes were given the names Big and Little Endian by Danny Cohen, in a whimsical reference to *Gulliver's Travels*, where the issue is which end of a boiled egg should be opened [HP95, Chapter 3.4].

---

[11] In this case, they differ by about a factor of 2, since 2^{-23} is even closer to 10^{-7}.

Chapter 5

Rounding

We saw in the previous chapter that the finite IEEE floating point numbers can all be expressed in the form
$$\pm(b_0.b_1b_2\ldots b_{p-1})_2 \times 2^E,$$
where p is the precision of the floating point system with, for normalized numbers, $b_0 = 1$ and $E_{\min} \leq E \leq E_{\max}$ and, for subnormal numbers and zero, $b_0 = 0$ and $E = E_{\min}$. We denoted the largest normalized number by $N_{\max}$ and the smallest positive normalized number by $N_{\min}$. There are also two infinite floating point numbers, $\pm\infty$.

We now introduce a new definition. We say that a real number x is in the *normalized range* of the floating point system if
$$N_{\min} \leq |x| \leq N_{\max}.$$
The numbers ± 0 and $\pm\infty$ and the subnormal numbers are not in the normalized range of the floating point system, although they are all valid floating point numbers.

Suppose that a real number x is not a floating point number. Then at least one (and perhaps both) of the following must be true:

- x is outside the normalized range (its absolute value is greater than $N_{\max}$ or less than $N_{\min}$). For example, the numbers 2^{130} and 2^{-130} are both outside the normalized range of the single format.

- The binary expansion of x requires more than p bits to specify the number exactly; equivalently, the floating point precision p is too small to represent x exactly. For example, the number
$$1 + 2^{-25} = (1.0000000000000000000000001)_2$$
requires more bits to specify it than are available in the significand field of the single format.

In either case, we need to approximate x by something else.

Let us define x_- to be the floating point number closest to x that is *less than or equal to* x, and define x_+ to be the floating point number closest to x that is *greater than or equal to* x. If the closest number is zero, we set the sign of zero to be the sign of x. For example, consider the toy floating point number system again. If $x = 1.7$, then $x_- = 1.5$ and $x_+ = 1.75$, as shown in Figure 5.1.

Returning to the IEEE floating point formats, let x be a positive number in the normalized range, and write x in the normalized form
$$x = (1.b_1b_2\ldots b_{p-1}b_pb_{p+1}\ldots)_2 \times 2^E. \tag{5.1}$$

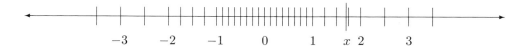

Figure 5.1: Rounding in the Toy System

It follows that the closest floating point number less than or equal to x is

$$x_- = (1.b_1b_2\ldots b_{p-1})_2 \times 2^E;$$

i.e., x_- is obtained by truncating the binary expansion of the significand, discarding b_p, b_{p+1}, etc. If x is not a floating point number, i.e., at least one of the discarded bits in its expansion is nonzero, then

$$x_+ = ((1.b_1b_2\ldots b_{p-1})_2 + (0.00\ldots 01)_2) \times 2^E,$$

the next floating point number bigger than x_-, and therefore also the next one that is bigger than x (which must lie between x_- and x_+). Here the "1" in the increment is in the $(p-1)$th place after the binary point, so the gap between x_- and x_+ is

$$2^{-(p-1)} \times 2^E. \tag{5.2}$$

Note that this quantity is the same as $\mathrm{ulp}(x_-)$, defined in (3.6). Finding the binary expansion of x_+ is a little more complicated, since one bit must be added to the last place of the fraction field of x_-; this may involve some "carries" and possibly, if all the bits in the field are 1, an increment in the exponent field.

If x is greater than $N_{\max}$, then

$$x_- = N_{\max} \quad \text{and} \quad x_+ = \infty.$$

If x is positive but less than $N_{\min}$, then x_- is either subnormal or zero, and x_+ is either subnormal or $N_{\min}$.

If x is negative, the situation just described is reversed. For example, if x is negative and in the normalized range, x_+ is obtained by dropping bits b_p, b_{p+1}, etc., since discarding bits of a negative number makes the number closer to zero, and therefore larger (further to the right on the real line). If x is negative but its absolute value is less than $N_{\min}$, then x_+ is either a negative subnormal number or -0, and x_- is either a negative subnormal number or $-N_{\min}$.

Correctly Rounded Values

The IEEE standard defines the *correctly rounded value of x*, which we shall denote by $\mathrm{round}(x)$, as follows. If x is a floating point number, then $\mathrm{round}(x) = x$. Otherwise, the correctly rounded value depends on which of the following four *rounding modes* is in effect:

- *Round down* (sometimes called round towards $-\infty$).
  $\mathrm{round}(x) = x_-$.

- *Round up* (sometimes called round towards ∞).
  $\mathrm{round}(x) = x_+$.

- *Round towards zero.*
  round(x) = x_- if $x > 0$; round(x) = x_+ if $x < 0$.

- *Round to nearest.*
  round(x) is either x_- or x_+, whichever is nearer to x (unless $|x| > N_{\max}$). In case of a tie, the one with its *least significant bit equal to zero* is chosen. See below for details.

If x is positive, then x_- is between zero and x, so *round down* and *round towards zero* have the same effect. If x is negative, then x_+ is between zero and x, so *round up* and *round towards zero* have the same effect. In both cases, *round towards zero* simply requires truncating the binary expansion, unless x is outside the normalized range.

The rounding mode that is almost always used in practice is *round to nearest*. In the toy system, *round to nearest* gives round(1.7) = 1.75 (see Figure 5.1). Consider x given by (5.1) again. If the first bit that cannot be stored, b_p, is 0, *round to nearest* rounds down to x_-; on the other hand, if $b_p = 1$ and at least one other subsequent nonzero bit is also 1, *round to nearest* rounds up to x_+. If $b_p = 1$ and all subsequent bits are 0, there is a tie. The least significant bits, i.e., the $(p-1)$th bits after the binary point, of x_- and x_+ must be different, and the one for which this bit equals 0 is chosen to break the tie. For the motivation for this rule, see [Go91, Theorem 5]. When the word *round* is used without any mention of a rounding mode, it almost always means *round to nearest*. The IEEE standard requires that the default rounding mode be *round to nearest*.

There is an exception to the *round to nearest* rule when $x > N_{\max}$. In this case, round(x) is defined to be $N_{\max}$ if $x < N_{\max} + \mathrm{ulp}(N_{\max})/2$ and ∞ otherwise. From a strictly mathematical point of view, this is not consistent with the usual definition, since x cannot be said to be closer to ∞ than to $N_{\max}$. From a practical point of view, however, the choice ∞ is important, since *round to nearest* is the default rounding mode and rounding to $N_{\max}$ may give very misleading results. Similar considerations apply when $x < -N_{\max}$.

Exercise 5.1 *What are the IEEE single format binary representations for the rounded value of $1/10$ (see (2.3)), using each of the four rounding modes? What are they for $1 + 2^{-25}$ and 2^{130}?*

Exercise 5.2 *Using the IEEE single format, construct an example where x_- and x_+ are the same distance from x, and use the tie-breaking rule to define round(x), assuming the round-to-nearest mode is in effect.*

Exercise 5.3 *Suppose that $0 < x < N_{\min}$, but that x is not a subnormal floating point number. We can write*

$$x = (0.b_1 b_2 \ldots b_{p-1} b_p b_{p+1} \ldots)_2 \times 2^{E_{\min}},$$

where at least one of $b_p, b_{p+1}, \ldots$, is not zero. What is x_-? Give some examples, assuming the single format is in use ($p = 24$, $E_{\min} = -126$).

Absolute Rounding Error and Ulp

We now define rounding error. Let x be a real number and let

$$\mathrm{abserr}(x) = |\mathrm{round}(x) - x|, \tag{5.3}$$

the *absolute rounding error* associated with x. Its value depends on the precision and rounding mode in effect. In toy precision, when *round down* or *round towards zero* is in effect, we have round$(1.7) = 1.5$, so

$$\text{abserr}(1.7) = 0.2,$$

but if *round up* or *round to nearest* is in effect, we have round$(1.7) = 1.75$, so

$$\text{abserr}(1.7) = 0.05.$$

Returning again to the IEEE formats, if x is in the normalized range, with

$$x = \pm(1.b_1b_2\ldots b_{p-1}b_pb_{p+1}\ldots)_2 \times 2^E, \tag{5.4}$$

the absolute rounding error associated with x is *less than the gap between x_- and x_+*, regardless of the rounding mode, and we have from (5.2) that

$$\text{abserr}(x) = |\text{round}(x) - x| < 2^{-(p-1)} \times 2^E. \tag{5.5}$$

Informally, we say that the absolute rounding error is less than one *ulp*, meaning ulp(x_-) if $x > 0$ and ulp(x_+) if $x < 0$. When *round to nearest* is in effect, we can say something stronger: the absolute rounding error is *less than or equal to half the gap between x_- and x_+*, i.e.,

$$\text{abserr}(x) = |\text{round}(x) - x| \leq 2^{-p} \times 2^E. \tag{5.6}$$

Informally, we say that the absolute rounding error is at most *half an ulp*. By definition, the absolute rounding error is zero when x is a floating point number.

Exercise 5.4 *What is* abserr$(1/10)$ *using the IEEE single format, for each of the four rounding modes? (See Exercise 5.1.)*

Exercise 5.5 *Suppose that $x > N_{\max}$. What is* abserr(x), *for each of the four rounding modes? Look carefully at the definition of* round(x).

Exercise 5.6 *What is* abserr(x) *for x given in Exercise 5.3, using the rounding mode round down?*

Exercise 5.7 *Do the bounds (5.5) and (5.6) hold when $|x| < N_{\min}$? Explain.*

Relative Rounding Error, Machine Epsilon, Significant Digits

The *relative rounding error* associated with a nonzero number x is defined by

$$\text{relerr}(x) = |\delta|, \tag{5.7}$$

where

$$\delta = \frac{\text{round}(x)}{x} - 1 = \frac{\text{round}(x) - x}{x}. \tag{5.8}$$

Assuming that x, given by (5.4), is in the normalized range and is not a floating point number, we have

$$|x| > 2^E. \tag{5.9}$$

Therefore, for all rounding modes, the relative rounding error satisfies the bound

$$\text{relerr}(x) = |\delta| = \frac{|\text{round}(x) - x|}{|x|} < \frac{2^{-(p-1)} \times 2^E}{2^E} = 2^{-(p-1)} = \epsilon, \tag{5.10}$$

CHAPTER 5. ROUNDING

using (5.5), (5.9), and the definition of ϵ in (3.5). In the case of *round to nearest*, we have
$$\text{relerr}(x) = |\delta| = \frac{|\text{round}(x) - x|}{|x|} < \frac{2^{-p} \times 2^E}{2^E} = 2^{-p} = \frac{1}{2}\epsilon, \tag{5.11}$$
using (5.6) and (5.9). The same inequalities hold when x is a floating point number in the normalized range, since then $\text{relerr}(x) = \text{abserr}(x) = 0$.

Exercise 5.8 *Do the bounds (5.10) and (5.11) hold when $|x| < N_{\min}$? Explain. (See Exercise 5.7.)*

It follows from (5.10) and (5.11) that
$$-\log_2 \text{relerr}(x) > p - 1$$
and, for *round to nearest*,
$$-\log_2 \text{relerr}(x) > p.$$
We can think of $-\log_2 \text{relerr}(x)$ as measuring the *number of bits* to which $\text{round}(x)$ and x agree: at least $p - 1$, and at least p in the case of *round to nearest*. Likewise, it follows from (5.10) that
$$-\log_{10} \text{relerr}(x) > -\log_{10}(\epsilon),$$
and we can think of $-\log_{10} \text{relerr}(x)$ as measuring the *number of decimal digits* to which $\text{round}(x)$ and x agree. Consulting Table 4.4 for the value of ϵ, we see that this means that $\text{round}(x)$ and x agree to at least about 7 digits when IEEE single precision is in use, and to about 16 digits in the case of IEEE double.

It also follows from (5.8) that
$$\text{round}(x) = x(1 + \delta).$$
Combining this with (5.10) and (5.11), we have completed the proof of the following result, which is so important that we state it as the only theorem in this book.

Theorem 5.1 *Let x be any real number in the normalized range of a binary floating point system with precision p. Then*
$$\text{round}(x) = x(1 + \delta)$$
for some δ satisfying
$$|\delta| < \epsilon,$$
where ϵ, machine epsilon, is the gap between 1 and the next larger floating point number, i.e.,
$$\epsilon = 2^{-(p-1)}.$$
Furthermore, if the rounding mode in effect is round to nearest,
$$|\delta| < \frac{1}{2}\epsilon = 2^{-p}.$$

Theorem 5.1 is very important, because it shows that, no matter how x is stored or displayed, either in binary format or in a converted decimal format, we may think of its value not as *exact* but as *exact within a factor* of $1 + \epsilon$. Thus, for example, IEEE single format numbers are accurate to within a factor of about $1 + 10^{-7}$, which means that they have approximately seven significant decimal digits.

Exercise 5.9 *Does the result established by Theorem 5.1 still hold if $0 < |x| < N_{\min}$? If not, give an x for which the conclusion is false.*

Chapter 6

Correctly Rounded Floating Point Operations

A key feature of the IEEE standard is that it requires correctly rounded operations, specifically:

- correctly rounded arithmetic operations (add, subtract, multiply, divide);
- correctly rounded remainder and square root operations;
- correctly rounded format conversions.

Correctly rounded means[12] rounded to fit the *destination* of the result, using the rounding mode in effect. For example, if the operation is the addition of two floating point numbers that are stored in registers, the destination for the result is normally one of these registers (overwriting one of the operands). On the other hand, the operation might be a store instruction, in which case the destination is a location in memory and a format conversion may be required. Regardless of whether the destination is a register or a memory location, its format could be IEEE single, double, or extended, depending on the machine being used and the program being executed.

Correctly Rounded Arithmetic

We begin by discussing the arithmetic operations. Very often, the result of an arithmetic operation on two floating point numbers is *not* a floating point number in the destination format. This is most obviously the case for multiplication and division; for example, 1 and 10 are both floating point numbers but we have already seen that $1/10$ is not, regardless of the destination format. It is also true of addition and subtraction: for example, 1 and 2^{-24} are IEEE single format numbers, but $1 + 2^{-24}$ is not.

Let x and y be floating point numbers, let $+, -, \times, /$ denote the four standard arithmetic operations, and let $\oplus, \ominus, \otimes, \oslash$ denote the corresponding operations as they are actually implemented on the computer. Thus, $x + y$ may not be a floating point number, but $x \oplus y$ is the floating point number that is the computed approximation of $x + y$. Before the development of the IEEE standard, the results of a floating point operation might be different on two different computers. Occasionally, the results could be quite bizarre. Consider the following questions, where in each case we assume

---

[12] On some systems, a precision mode allows rounding to a precision narrower than that provided by the destination. See Chapter 8.

that the destination for the result has the same format as the floating point numbers x and y.

Question 6.1 *If x is a floating point number, is the floating point product $1 \otimes x$ equal to x?*

Question 6.2 *If x is a nonzero (and finite) floating point number, is the floating point quotient $x \oslash x$ equal to 1?*

Question 6.3 *If x is a floating point number, is the floating point product $0.5 \otimes x$ the same as the floating point quotient $x \oslash 2$?*

Question 6.4 *If x and y are floating point numbers, and the floating point difference $x \ominus y$ is zero, does x equal y?*

Normally, the answer to all these questions would be *yes*, but for each of Questions 6.1 through 6.3, there was a widely used computer in the 1960s or 1970s for which the answer was *no* for some input x [Sev98], [Kah00], [PH97, Section 4.12]. These anomalies *cannot* occur with IEEE arithmetic. As for Question 6.4, virtually all systems developed before the standard were such that the answer could be *no* for small enough values of x and y; on some systems, the answer could be *no* even if x and y were both near 1 (see the discussion following equation (6.4)). With IEEE arithmetic, the answer to Question 6.4 is always *yes*; see the next chapter.

When the result of a floating point operation is not a floating point number in the destination format, the IEEE standard requires that the computed result be the rounded value of the exact result, i.e., rounded to fit the destination, using the rounding mode in effect. It is worth stating this requirement carefully. The rule is as follows: if x and y are floating point numbers, then

$$x \oplus y = \text{round}(x + y),$$
$$x \ominus y = \text{round}(x - y),$$
$$x \otimes y = \text{round}(x \times y),$$

and

$$x \oslash y = \text{round}(x/y),$$

where round is the operation of rounding to the given destination, using the rounding mode in effect.

Exercise 6.1 *Show that the IEEE rule of correctly rounded arithmetic immediately guarantees that the answers to Questions 6.1 to 6.3 must be yes. Show further that no rounding is necessary, i.e., that the exact result is a floating point number except in one specific case; what is that case?*

Using Theorem 5.1, it follows that, as long as $x + y$ is in the normalized range,

$$x \oplus y = (x + y)(1 + \delta),$$

where

$$|\delta| < \epsilon,$$

machine epsilon for the destination format. This applies to all rounding modes; for *round to nearest*, we have the stronger result

$$|\delta| < \frac{1}{2}\epsilon.$$

CHAPTER 6. CORRECTLY ROUNDED FLOATING POINT OPERATIONS

For example, if the destination format is IEEE single and the rounding mode is *round to nearest*, floating point addition is accurate to within a factor of $1 + 2^{-24}$, i.e., to approximately seven decimal digits. The same holds for the other operations $\ominus$, $\otimes$, and $\oslash$.

Exercise 6.2 *Suppose that the destination format is IEEE single and the rounding mode is* round to nearest. *What are* $64 \oplus 2^{20}$, $64 \oplus 2^{-20}$, $32 \oplus 2^{-20}$, $16 \oplus 2^{-20}$, $8 \oplus 2^{-20}$? *Give your answers in binary, not decimal. What are the results if the rounding mode is changed to* round up?

Exercise 6.3 *Recalling how many decimal digits correspond to the 24-bit precision of an IEEE single format number, which of the following expressions do you think have the value exactly 1 if the destination format is IEEE single and the rounding mode is* round to nearest: $1 \oplus \text{round}(10^{-5})$, $1 \oplus \text{round}(10^{-10})$, $1 \oplus \text{round}(10^{-15})$?

Exercise 6.4 *What is the largest floating point number x for which $1 \oplus x$ is exactly 1, assuming the destination format is IEEE single and the rounding mode is* round to nearest? *What if the destination format is IEEE double?*

The result of a sequence of *two or more* arithmetic operations may *not* be the correctly rounded value of the exact result. For example, consider the computation of $(x + y) - z$, where $x = 1$, $y = 2^{-25}$, and $z = 1$, assuming the destination format for both operations is IEEE single, and with *round to nearest* in effect. The numbers x, y, and z are all IEEE single format floating point numbers, since $x = z = 1.0 \times 2^0$ and $y = 1.0 \times 2^{-25}$. The exact sum of the first two numbers is

$$x + y = 1.00000000000000000000000001.$$

This does not fit the single format, so it is rounded, giving

$$x \oplus y = 1.$$

The final result is therefore

$$(x \oplus y) \ominus z = 1 \ominus 1 = 0.$$

However, the exact result is

$$(x + y) - z = 2^{-25},$$

which *does* fit the single format exactly. Notice that the exact result would be obtained if the destination format for the intermediate result $x + y$ is the IEEE double or extended format (see Chapter 8).

Exercise 6.5 *In this example, what is $x \oplus (y \ominus z)$, and $(x \ominus z) \oplus y$, assuming the destination format for all operations is IEEE single?*

Exercise 6.6 *Using the same example, what is $(x \oplus y) \ominus z$ if the rounding mode is* round up?

Exercise 6.7 *Let $x = 1$, $y = 2^{-15}$, and $z = 2^{15}$, stored in the single format. What is $(x \oplus y) \oplus z$, when the destination format for both operations is the single format, using* round to nearest? *What if the rounding mode is* round up?

Exercise 6.8 *In exact arithmetic, the addition operation is commutative, i.e.,*

$$x + y = y + x$$

for any two numbers x, y, and also associative, i.e.,

$$x + (y + z) = (x + y) + z$$

for any x, y, and z. Is the floating point addition operation $\oplus$ commutative? Is it associative?

The availability of the rounding modes *round down* and *round up* allows a programmer to make any individual computation twice, once with each mode. The two results define an interval that must contain the exact result. *Interval arithmetic* is the name used when sequences of computations are done in this way. See Exercises 10.17, 10.18, 13.5, and 13.11.

Addition and Subtraction

Now we ask the question: How is correctly rounded arithmetic implemented? This is surprisingly complicated. Let us consider the addition of two IEEE single format floating point numbers $x = S \times 2^E$ and $y = T \times 2^F$, assuming the destination format for $x+y$ is also IEEE single. If the two exponents E and F are the same, it is necessary only to add the significands S and T. The final result is $(S + T) \times 2^E$, which then needs further normalization if $S + T$ is greater than or equal to 2, or less than 1. For example, the result of adding $3 = (1.100)_2 \times 2^1$ to $2 = (1.000)_2 \times 2^1$ is

$$
\begin{array}{rl}
 & (\ 1.10000000000000000000000\ )_2 \times 2^1 \\
+ & (\ 1.00000000000000000000000\ )_2 \times 2^1 \\
= & (10.10000000000000000000000\ )_2 \times 2^1 \\
\text{Normalize}: & (\ 1.01000000000000000000000\ )_2 \times 2^2.
\end{array}
$$

However, if the two exponents E and F are different, say with $E > F$, the first step in adding the two numbers is to *align the significands*, shifting T right $E - F$ positions so that the second number is no longer normalized and both numbers have the same exponent E. The significands are then added as before. For example, adding $3 = (1.100)_2 \times 2^1$ to $3/4 = (1.100)_2 \times 2^{-1}$ gives

$$
\begin{array}{rl}
 & (\ 1.10000000000000000000000\ )_2 \times 2^1 \\
+ & (\ 0.01100000000000000000000\ )_2 \times 2^1 \\
= & (\ 1.11100000000000000000000\ )_2 \times 2^1.
\end{array}
$$

In this case, the result does not need further normalization.

Guard Bits

Now consider adding 3 to 3×2^{-23}. We get

$$
\begin{array}{rl}
 & (\ 1.10000000000000000000000\ \ \ )_2 \times 2^1 \\
+ & (\ 0.00000000000000000000000|1\ )_2 \times 2^1 \\
= & (\ 1.10000000000000000000000|1\ )_2 \times 2^1 \qquad (6.1) \\
\text{Round Down}: & (\ 1.10000000000000000000000\ \ \ )_2 \times 2^1 \\
\text{or Round Up}: & (\ 1.10000000000000000000001\ \ \ )_2 \times 2^1.
\end{array}
$$

CHAPTER 6. CORRECTLY ROUNDED FLOATING POINT OPERATIONS

This time, the result is not an IEEE single format floating point number, since its significand has 24 bits after the binary point: the 24th is shown beyond the vertical bar. Therefore, the result must be *correctly rounded*. In the case of rounding to nearest, there is a tie, so the result with its final bit equal to zero is used (round up in this case).

Rounding should not take place before the result is normalized. Consider the example of subtracting the floating point number $1+2^{-22}+2^{-23}$ from 3, or equivalently adding 3 and $-(1+2^{-22}+2^{-23})$. We get

$$
\begin{aligned}
& (\ 1.10000000000000000000000\ )_2 \times 2^1 \\
-\ & (\ 0.10000000000000000000001|1\ )_2 \times 2^1 \\
=\ & (\ 0.11111111111111111111110|1\ )_2 \times 2^1 \\
\text{Normalize:}\ & (\ 1.11111111111111111111101\ )_2 \times 2^0.
\end{aligned}
\qquad (6.2)
$$

Thus, rounding is not needed in this example.

In both examples (6.1) and (6.2), it was necessary to *carry out the operation using an extra bit*, called a *guard bit*, shown after the vertical line following the b_{23} position. Without the guard bit, the correctly rounded result would not have been obtained.

Exercise 6.9 *Work out the details for the examples $1 + 2^{-24}$ and $1 - 2^{-24}$. Make up some more examples where a guard bit is required.*

The following is a particularly interesting example. Consider computing $x - y$ with $x = (1.0)_2 \times 2^0$ and $y = (1.1111\ldots1)_2 \times 2^{-1}$, where the fraction field for y contains 23 ones after the binary point. (Note that y is only slightly smaller than x; in fact, it is the next floating point number smaller than x.) Aligning the significands, we obtain

$$
\begin{aligned}
& (\ 1.00000000000000000000000|\ )_2 \times 2^0 \\
-\ & (\ 0.11111111111111111111111|1\ )_2 \times 2^0 \\
=\ & (\ 0.00000000000000000000000|1\ )_2 \times 2^0 \\
\text{Normalize:}\ & (\ 1.00000000000000000000000|0\ )_2 \times 2^{-24}.
\end{aligned}
\qquad (6.3)
$$

This is an example of *cancellation*, since almost all the bits in the two numbers cancel each other. The result is $(1.0)_2 \times 2^{-24}$, which is a floating point number. As in the previous example, we need a guard bit to get the correct answer; indeed, without it, we would get a completely wrong answer.

The following example shows that more than one guard bit may be necessary. Consider computing $x - y$ where $x = 1.0$ and $y = (1.000\ldots01)_2 \times 2^{-25}$, where y has 22 zero bits between the binary point and the final 1 bit. Using 25 guard bits, we get

$$
\begin{aligned}
& (\ 1.00000000000000000000000|\ )_2 \times 2^0 \\
-\ & (\ 0.00000000000000000000000|0100000000000000000000001\ )_2 \times 2^0 \\
=\ & (\ 0.11111111111111111111111|1011111111111111111111111\ )_2 \times 2^0 \\
\text{Normalize:}\ & (\ 1.11111111111111111111111|0111111111111111111111110\ )_2 \times 2^{-1} \\
\text{Round to}\ & \\
\text{Nearest:}\ & (\ 1.11111111111111111111111\ )_2 \times 2^{-1}.
\end{aligned}
$$

This is the correctly rounded value of the exact sum of the numbers. If we were to use only two guard bits, we would get the result:

$$
\begin{aligned}
&(\ 1.00000000000000000000000| \ )_2 \times 2^0 \\
- \ &(\ 0.00000000000000000000000|01 \ )_2 \times 2^0 \\
= \ &(\ 0.11111111111111111111111|11 \ )_2 \times 2^0 \\
\text{Normalize}: \ &(\ 1.11111111111111111111111|1 \ )_2 \times 2^{-1} \\
\text{Round to Nearest}: \ &(\ 10.0000000000000000000000 \ )_2 \times 2^{-1} \\
\text{Renormalize}: \ &(\ 1.00000000000000000000000 \ )_2 \times 2^0.
\end{aligned}
$$

In this case, normalizing and rounding results in rounding up (using the tie-breaking rule) instead of down, giving the final result 1.0, which is *not* the correctly rounded value of the exact sum. We get the same wrong answer even if we have 3, 4, or as many as 24 guard bits in this case! Machines that implement correctly rounded arithmetic take such possibilities into account. However, by being a little clever, the need for 25 guard bits can be avoided. Let us repeat the same example, with two guard bits, but with one additional bit "turned on" to indicate that at least one nonzero extra bit was discarded when the bits of the second number, y, were shifted to the right past the second guard bit position. The bit is called *sticky* because once it is turned on, it stays on, regardless of how many bits are discarded. Now, before doing the subtraction, we put the sticky bit in a third guard bit position. For this example, we then get

$$
\begin{aligned}
&(\ 1.00000000000000000000000| \ )_2 \times 2^0 \\
- \ &(\ 0.00000000000000000000000|011 \ )_2 \times 2^0 \\
= \ &(\ 0.11111111111111111111111|101 \ )_2 \times 2^0 \\
\text{Normalize}: \ &(\ 1.11111111111111111111111|01 \ )_2 \times 2^{-1} \\
\text{Round to Nearest}: \ &(\ 1.11111111111111111111111 \ )_2 \times 2^{-1},
\end{aligned}
$$

which is the correct answer. In general, it is necessary to use only three extra bits to implement correctly rounded floating point addition and subtraction: two guard bits (often called the guard and round bits) and one sticky bit [Gol95].

Exercise 6.10 *Consider the operation $x + y$, where $x = 1.0$ and $y = (1.000\ldots01)_2 \times 2^{-24}$, and y has 22 zero bits between the binary point and the final 1 bit. What is the correctly rounded result, assuming* round to nearest *is in use? What is computed if only one guard bit is used? What if two guard bits are used? What if two guard bits and a sticky bit are used?*

When the IBM 360 was released in 1965, it did not have any guard bits, and it was only after the strenuous objections of computer scientists that later versions of the machine incorporated one hexadecimal guard digit—still not enough to guarantee correctly rounded arithmetic. Decades later, the Cray supercomputer still did not have a guard bit. Let $x = 1$ and let y be the next floating point number smaller than 1, and consider the operation $x - y$, as in example (6.3) above. On one Cray machine, the computed result $x \ominus y$ is wrong by a factor of 2, since a 1 is shifted past the end of the second operand's significand and discarded. Thus we have

$$x \ominus y = 2(x - y) \quad \text{instead of } x \ominus y = (x - y)(1 + \delta), \quad \text{where } |\delta| \leq \epsilon. \tag{6.4}$$

On another Cray machine, the second operand y is rounded before the operation takes place. This converts the second operand to the value 1.0 and gives the result $x \ominus y = 0$, so that in this case the answer to Question 6.4 is *no*, even though x and y are not small numbers.

Multiplication and Division

Floating point multiplication and division, unlike addition and subtraction, do not require significands to be aligned. If $x = S \times 2^E$ and $y = T \times 2^F$, then

$$x \times y = (S \times T) \times 2^{E+F},$$

so there are three steps to floating point multiplication: multiply the significands, add the exponents, and normalize and correctly round the result. Likewise, division requires taking the quotient of the significands and the difference of the exponents. However, multiplication and division of the significands are substantially more complicated operations than addition and subtraction. In principle it is possible, by using enough space on the chip, to implement the operations so that they are all equally fast. In practice, chip designers build the hardware so that multiplication is approximately as fast as addition, because in many floating point applications addition and multiplication appear together in the inner loop. However, the division operation, which is the most complicated to implement, generally takes significantly longer to execute than addition or multiplication. Division by zero will be discussed in the next chapter.

Exercise 6.11 *Assume that $x = S \times 2^E$ and $y = T \times 2^F$ are normalized floating point numbers, i.e., $1 \leq |S| < 2$, $1 \leq |T| < 2$, with (the binary representations of) S and T each having p bits (including the hidden bit). Let U be the exact product of the two significands, i.e., $U = S \times T$.*

1. *What are the possibilities for the number of nonzero bits to the left of the binary point of (the binary representation for) U? What does this tell you about how many bits it may be necessary to shift the binary point of U left or right to normalize the result?*

2. *What are the possibilities for the number of nonzero bits to the right of the binary point of U? In what cases can U be represented exactly using p bits (including the hidden bit), and in what cases must the result be rounded to fit a p-bit destination?*

Exercise 6.12 *The pigeon-hole principle (J. Demmel, W. Kahan; see also [Ede94]). Answer the following questions for (a) the toy floating point system shown in Figures 3.1 and 4.1, and (b) the IEEE single format numbers.*

1. *How many floating point numbers x satisfy $1 \leq x < 2$? How many of these satisfy $1 \leq x < 3/2$ and how many satisfy $3/2 \leq x < 2$?*

2. *How many floating point numbers x satisfy $1/2 < x \leq 1$? Approximately how many of these satisfy $1/2 < x \leq 2/3$ and approximately how many satisfy $2/3 < x \leq 1$?*

3. *Does it follow that there must exist two different floating point numbers x_1 and x_2 between 1 and 2 for which the computed reciprocals $1 \oslash x_1$ and $1 \oslash x_2$ are the same (rounded to the same format)? Are you thinking of x_1 and x_2 between 1 and 3/2 or between 3/2 and 2? Is this true regardless of the rounding mode?*

4. *Does it follow that there exist floating point numbers x for which*

$$(1 \oslash x) \otimes x$$

is not exactly 1? Is this true regardless of the rounding mode? Does it also follow that there exist floating point numbers x for which

$$1 \oslash (1 \oslash x)$$

is not exactly x?

The Intel Pentium chip received a lot of bad publicity in 1994 when the fact that it had a floating point hardware bug was exposed. An example of the bug's effects is that, on the original Pentium, the floating point division operation

$$\frac{4195835}{3145727}$$

gave a result with only about 4 correct decimal digits. The error occurred in only a few special cases and could easily have remained undiscovered much longer than it did; it was found by a mathematician doing experiments in number theory. Nonetheless, it created a sensation, mainly because it turned out that Intel knew about the bug but had not released the information. The public outcry against incorrect floating point arithmetic depressed Intel's stock value significantly until the company finally agreed to replace everyone's defective processors, not just those belonging to institutions that Intel thought really needed correct arithmetic! It is hard to imagine a more effective way to persuade the public that floating point accuracy is important than to inform it that only specialists can have it. The event was particularly ironic since no company had done more than Intel to make accurate floating point available to the masses. For details on how the bug arose, see [Ede97].

For more on how computers implement arithmetic operations, see [HP95, PH97, Gol95]. For a wealth of information on rounding properties of floating point arithmetic at a more advanced level, see Goldberg [Gol91] and Kahan [Kah97, Kah96b, Kah00].

Remainder, Square Root, and Format Conversions

In addition to requiring that the basic arithmetic operations be correctly rounded, the IEEE standard also requires that correctly rounded remainder and square root operations be provided. The remainder operation, x REM y, is valid for finite x and nonzero y and produces $r = x - y \times n$, where n is the integer nearest the exact value x/y. The square root operation is valid for all nonnegative arguments. The standard method for computing square roots goes back to Newton.

Exercise 6.13 *The formula for the length of the hypotenuse of a right-angled triangle is*

$$z = \sqrt{x^2 + y^2},$$

where x and y are the lengths of the legs of the triangle. Suppose this formula is computed using IEEE floating point arithmetic when it happens that all of x, y, and z are integers (e.g., 3, 4, and 5 or 5, 12, and 13). Will the floating point result for z necessarily be an integer?

Numbers are usually input to the computer using some kind of high-level programming language, to be processed by a compiler or an interpreter. There are two different ways that a number such as 1/10 might be input. One way would be to input the decimal string 0.1 directly, either in the program itself or in the input to the program. The compiler or interpreter then calls a standard input-handling procedure which generates machine instructions to convert the decimal string to a binary format and store the correctly rounded result in memory or a register. Alternatively, the integers 1 and 10 might be input to the program and the ratio 1/10 generated by a division operation. In this case too, the input-handling procedure must be called to read the integer strings 1 and 10 and convert them to binary representation. Either integer or floating point format might be used to store these values, depending on the type of the variables used in the program, but the values must be converted to floating point format before the division operation computes the quotient 1/10.

Just as decimal to binary conversion is typically needed to input data to the computer, binary to decimal conversion is usually needed to output results when computation is completed.

The standard requires support for correctly rounded format conversions. These fall into several categories:

- Conversion between floating point formats. Conversion from a narrower to a wider precision (e.g., from single to double) must be exact. Conversion from a wider precision to a narrower one requires correct rounding.

- Conversion between floating point and integer formats. Conversion from a floating point format to an integer format requires rounding to the nearest integer using the rounding mode in effect. If the floating point number is already an integer, the conversion should be exact unless this number does not fit the integer format. Conversion from integer format to floating point format may require rounding (see Exercise 3.10).[13]

- Rounding a floating point number to an integral value. This is also a required feature, so that rounding to an integral value does not require use of the integer format.

- Binary to decimal and decimal to binary conversion. The rounding mode is used to round these conversions. There is an important requirement when *round to nearest* is in effect: if a binary single format number is converted to at least 9 decimal digits and then converted from this decimal representation back to the binary single format, the original number must be recovered. The same rule holds for the double format, using at least 17 decimal digits. This double format conversion requirement was one motivation for the precision specifications for the extended format discussed in Chapter 4 [Gol91]. IEEE 754 does not require correctly rounded conversions in all cases, because efficient algorithms to do so were not known in 1985. However, the technology has advanced since then, and efficient conversion algorithms that round correctly in all cases are now known [Gay90] and are implemented in widely used software available from [Net].

---

[13]This point is not actually made in IEEE 754, but is clarified in IEEE 854.

Chapter 7

Exceptions

One of the most difficult things about programming is the need to anticipate exceptional situations. Ideally, a program should handle exceptional data in a manner as consistent as possible with the handling of unexceptional data. For example, a program that reads integers from an input file and echoes them to an output file until the end of the input file is reached should not fail just because the input file is empty. On the other hand, if it is further required to compute the average value of the input data, no reasonable solution is available if the input file is empty. So it is with floating point arithmetic. When a reasonable response to exceptional data is possible, it should be used.

Infinity from Division by Zero

The simplest example of an exception is *division by zero*. Before the IEEE standard was devised, there were two standard responses to division of a positive number by zero. One often used in the 1950s was to generate the largest floating point number as the result. The rationale offered by the manufacturers was that the user would notice the large number in the output and draw the conclusion that something had gone wrong. However, this often led to confusion: for example, the expression $1/0 - 1/0$ would give the result 0, so the user might *not* notice that any error had taken place. Consequently, it was emphasized in the 1960s that division by zero should lead to the interruption or termination of the program, perhaps giving the user an informative message such as "fatal error—division by zero." To avoid this, the burden was on the programmer to make sure that division by zero would never occur.

Suppose, for example, it is desired to compute the total resistance of an electrical circuit with two resistors connected in parallel, with resistances, respectively, R_1 and R_2 ohms, as shown in Figure 7.1. The formula for the total resistance of the circuit is

$$T = \frac{1}{\frac{1}{R_1} + \frac{1}{R_2}}. \tag{7.1}$$

This formula makes intuitive sense: if both resistances R_1 and R_2 are the same value R, then the resistance of the whole circuit is $T = R/2$, since the current divides equally, with equal amounts flowing through each resistor. On the other hand, if R_1 is very much smaller than R_2, the resistance of the whole circuit is somewhat less than R_1, since most of the current flows through the first resistor and avoids the second one. What if R_1 is zero? The answer is intuitively clear: since the first resistor offers no resistance to the current, *all* the current flows through that resistor and avoids the second one; therefore, the total resistance in the circuit is zero. The formula for T

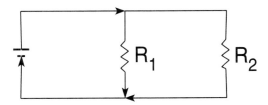

Figure 7.1: The Parallel Resistance Circuit

also makes sense mathematically if we introduce the convention that $1/0 = \infty$ and $1/\infty = 0$. We get

$$T = \frac{1}{\frac{1}{0} + \frac{1}{R_2}} = \frac{1}{\infty + \frac{1}{R_2}} = \frac{1}{\infty} = 0.$$

Why, then, should a programmer writing code for the evaluation of parallel resistance formulas have to worry about treating division by zero as an exceptional situation? In IEEE arithmetic, the programmer is relieved of that burden. The standard response to division by zero is to produce an infinite result and continue with program execution. In the case of the parallel resistance formula, this leads to the correct final result $1/\infty = 0$.

NaN from Invalid Operation

It is true that $a \times 0$ has the value 0 for any *finite* value of a. Similarly, we adopt the convention that $a/0 = \infty$ for any *positive* value of a. Multiplication with ∞ also makes sense: $a \times \infty$ has the value ∞ for any *positive* value of a. But the expressions $0 \times \infty$ and $0/0$ make no mathematical sense. An attempt to compute either of these quantities is called an *invalid operation*, and the IEEE standard response to such an operation is to set the result to NaN (Not a Number). Any subsequent arithmetic computation with an expression that involves a NaN also results in a NaN. When a NaN is discovered in the output of a program, the programmer knows something has gone wrong and can invoke debugging tools to determine what the problem is.

Addition with ∞ makes mathematical sense. In the parallel resistance example, we see that $\infty + \frac{1}{R_2} = \infty$. This is true even if R_2 also happens to be zero, because $\infty + \infty = \infty$. We also have $a - \infty = -\infty$ for any *finite* value of a. But there is no way to make sense of the expression $\infty - \infty$, which therefore yields the result NaN.

These conventions can be justified mathematically by considering addition of limits. Suppose there are two sequences x_k and y_k both diverging to ∞, e.g., $x_k = 2^k$, $y_k = 2k$, for $k = 1, 2, 3, \ldots$, or the other way around. Clearly, the sequence $x_k + y_k$ also diverges to ∞. This justifies the expression $\infty + \infty = \infty$. But it is impossible to make a statement about the limit of $x_k - y_k$, since the result depends on whether one of the sequences diverges faster than the other. Consequently, $\infty - \infty$ is NaN.

Exercise 7.1 *What are the values of the expressions $\infty/0$, $0/\infty$, and ∞/∞? Justify your answer.*

Exercise 7.2 *For what nonnegative values of a is it true that a/∞ equals zero?*

Exercise 7.3 *Using the 1950s convention for treatment of division by zero mentioned above, the expression $(1/0)/10000000$ results in a number very much smaller than the largest floating point number. What is the result in IEEE arithmetic?*

CHAPTER 7. EXCEPTIONS

Exercise 7.4 *The formula $R_1 R_2/(R_1 + R_2)$ is equivalent to (7.1), if R_1 and R_2 are both nonzero. Does it deliver the correct answer using IEEE arithmetic if R_1 or R_2, or both, are zero?*

Signed Zeros and Signed Infinities

A question arises: Why should $1/0$ have the value ∞ rather than $-\infty$? This is one motivation for the existence of the floating point number -0, so that the conventions $a/0 = \infty$ and $a/(-0) = -\infty$ may be followed, where a is a positive number. The reverse holds if a is negative. The predicate $0 = -0$ is true, but the predicate $\infty = -\infty$ is false. We are led to the conclusion that it is possible that the predicates $a = b$ and $1/a = 1/b$ have opposite values (the first true, the second false, if $a = 0$, $b = -0$). This phenomenon is a direct consequence of the convention for handling infinity.

The floating point number -0 is produced by several operations, including the unary operation -0, as well as a/∞ when a is negative, $a \times 0$ when a is negative, and the square root of -0, regardless of the rounding mode, as well as $a - a$ for any finite a when the rounding mode is *round down*. Not all programming environments display the sign of zero by default, because users rarely needs to distinguish between 0 and -0.

Exercise 7.5 *Are there any other cases in which the predicates $a = b$ and $1/a = 1/b$ have opposite values, besides a and b being zeros of opposite sign?*

Exercise 7.6 *What are the values of the expressions $0/(-0)$, $\infty/(-\infty)$, and $-\infty/(-0)$?*

Exercise 7.7 *What is the result for the parallel resistance formula (7.1) if $R_1 = 1$ and $R_2 = -0$?*

More about NaNs

The square root operation provides a good example of the use of NaNs. Before the IEEE standard, an attempt to take the square root of a negative number might result only in the printing of an error message and a positive result being returned. The user might not notice that anything had gone wrong. Under the rules of the IEEE standard, the square root operation is invalid if its argument is negative, and the standard response is to return a NaN. Likewise, the remainder operation a REM b is invalid if a is $\pm\infty$ or b is ± 0, and the standard response is to return a NaN.

More generally, NaNs provide a very convenient way for a programmer to handle the possibility of invalid data or other errors in many contexts. Suppose we wish to write a program to compute a function that is not defined for some input values. By setting the output of the function to NaN if the input is invalid or some other error takes place during the computation of the function, the need to return special error messages or codes is avoided. Another good use of NaNs is for initializing variables that are not otherwise assigned initial values when they are declared. Furthermore, the bitstring in the fraction field can, in principle at least, be used to code the origin of the NaN. Consequently, we do not speak of a unique NaN value but of many possible NaN values. The standard distinguishes quiet NaNs and signaling NaNs, but since signaling NaNs are rarely used in practice, we make no such distinction here.

When a and b are real numbers, one of three relational conditions holds: $a = b$, $a < b$, or $a > b$. The same is true if a and b are floating point numbers in the conventional sense, even if the values $\pm\infty$ are permitted. However, if either a or b is a NaN none of the three conditions $a = b$, $a < b$, $a > b$ can be said to hold (even if both a and b are NaNs). Instead, a and b are said to be *unordered*. Consequently, although the predicates $a \leq b$ and $(\text{not}(a > b))$ usually have the same value, they have *different* values (the first false, the second true) if either a or b is a NaN.

The conversion of a binary format floating point number to an integer or decimal representation that is too big for the format in question is an invalid operation, but it cannot deliver a NaN since there is no floating point destination for the result.

Exercise 7.8 *Extend Exercise* 4.3 *to the case where either x or y may be ± 0, $\pm \infty$, or NaN, and the result may be "unordered".*

Overflow

Traditionally, *overflow* is said to occur when the exact result of a floating point operation is finite but with an absolute value that is larger than the largest floating point number. As with division by zero, in the days before IEEE arithmetic was available the usual treatment of overflow was to set the result to (plus or minus) the largest floating point number or to interrupt or terminate the program. In IEEE arithmetic, the standard response to overflow is to deliver the correctly rounded result, either $\pm N_{\max}$ or $\pm \infty$. The range of numbers that round to $\pm \infty$ depends on the rounding mode; see Chapter 5.

To be precise, overflow is said to occur in IEEE arithmetic when the exact result of an operation is finite but so big that its correctly rounded value is different from what it would be if the exponent upper limit $E_{\max}$ were sufficiently large. In the case of *round to nearest*, this is the same as saying that overflow occurs when an exact finite result is rounded to $\pm \infty$, but it is not the same for the other rounding modes. For example, in the case of *round down* or *round towards zero*, if an exact finite result x is more than $N_{\max}$, it is rounded down to $N_{\max}$ no matter how large x is, but overflow is said to occur only if $x \geq N_{\max} + \text{ulp}(N_{\max})$, since otherwise the rounded value would be the same even if the exponent range were increased.

Gradual Underflow

Traditionally, *underflow* is said to occur when the exact result of an operation is nonzero but with an absolute value that is smaller than the smallest normalized floating point number. In the days before IEEE arithmetic, the response to underflow was typically, though not always, *flush to zero*: return the result 0. In IEEE arithmetic, the standard response to underflow is to return the correctly rounded value, which may be a subnormal number, ± 0 or $\pm N_{\min}$. This is known as *gradual underflow*. Gradual underflow was and still is the most controversial part of the IEEE standard. Its proponents argued (and still do) that its use provides many valuable arithmetic rounding properties and significantly adds to the reliability of floating point software. Its opponents argued (and still do) that arithmetic with subnormal numbers is too complicated to justify inclusion as a hardware operation which will be needed only occasionally. The ensuing debate accounted for much of the delay in the adoption of the IEEE standard. Even today, some IEEE compliant microprocessors support gradual underflow only in software. The standard gives several options for defining exactly when the underflow exception is said to occur; see [CKVV02] for details.

The motivation for gradual underflow can be summarized very simply: compare Figure 3.1 with Figure 4.1 to see how the use of subnormal numbers fills in the relatively large gap between $\pm N_{\min}$ and zero. The immediate consequence is that the worst case absolute rounding error for numbers that underflow to subnormal numbers is the *same* as the worst case absolute rounding error for numbers that round to $N_{\min}$. This is an obviously appealing property.

Consider the following subtraction operation, using the IEEE single format. The second operand is $N_{\min}$ and the first operand is a little bigger:

$$\begin{aligned}
& (1.01000000000000000000000 \;)_2 \times 2^{-126} \\
&-\; (1.00000000000000000000000 \;)_2 \times 2^{-126} \\
&=\; (0.01000000000000000000000 \;)_2 \times 2^{-126} \\
\text{Normalize}: & (1.00000000000000000000000 \;)_2 \times 2^{-128}.
\end{aligned} \qquad (7.2)$$

The last line shows the ideal normalized representation, but this is smaller than $N_{\min}$. Without gradual underflow, we would have to flush the result to zero, so that in this case the answer to Question 6.4 is *no*. With gradual underflow, the answer 2^{-128} can be stored exactly, with the subnormal representation

| 0 | 00000000 | 01000000000000000000000 |

This suggests that, when gradual underflow is supported, the answer to Question 6.4 is always *yes*. This is indeed the case; see Exercise 7.12.

Extensive analysis by Coonen [Coo81], Demmel [Dem84], and Kahan [Kah96b] makes a very convincing case for the value of gradual underflow. It is high time to bury this controversy and to accept gradual underflow as a clever yet practical solution to a tricky technical problem, and one that demands hardware support.

Exercise 7.9 *Using* round to nearest, *what numbers are rounded down to zero and what numbers are rounded up to the smallest subnormal number?*

Exercise 7.10 *Consider the operation*

$$(y \ominus x) \oplus x,$$

where the first part of the operation, $y \ominus x$, underflows. What is the result when gradual underflow is used? What is the result when flush to zero is used? Which correctly approximates the exact result? (See [Cod81].)

Exercise 7.11 *Suppose that x and y are floating point numbers with the property that*

$$\frac{1}{2} \leq \frac{x}{y} \leq 2.$$

Show that the exact difference $x-y$ is also a floating point number, so that $x \ominus y = x-y$, if gradual underflow is used. Show that this is not always the case if flush to zero is used. (See [Kah96b, Ste74].)

Exercise 7.12 *Prove that the answer to Question 6.4 is always yes in IEEE arithmetic, because of gradual underflow.*

Exercise 7.13 *Is the worst case relative rounding error for numbers that underflow to subnormal numbers the same as the worst case relative rounding error for numbers that round to $N_{\min}$? Why or why not?*

Table 7.1: IEEE Standard Response to Exceptions

Invalid Operation	Set result to NaN
Division by Zero	Set result to $\pm\infty$
Overflow	Set result to $\pm\infty$ or $\pm N_{\max}$
Underflow	Set result to ± 0, $\pm N_{\min}$ or subnormal
Inexact	Set result to correctly rounded value

The Five Exception Types

Altogether, the IEEE standard defines five kinds of exceptions: invalid operation, division by zero, overflow, underflow, and inexact, together with a *standard response* to each of these. All of these have now been described except the last. The inexact exception is, in fact, not exceptional at all because it occurs every time the result of an arithmetic operation is not a floating point number and therefore requires rounding. Table 7.1 summarizes the standard responses to the five exceptions.

The IEEE standard specifies that when an exception occurs it must be *signaled* by setting an associated *status flag*, and strongly recommends that the programmer should have the option of either *trapping the exception*, providing special code to be executed when the exception occurs, or *masking the exception*, in which case the program continues executing with the standard response shown in the table. The status flags are *sticky*, i.e., once a flag is set, it remains set until cleared. This allows the programmer to tell whether or not an exception occurred during execution of a given segment of code. If the user is not programming in assembly language, but in a higher level language being processed by an interpreter or a compiler, the ability to trap exceptions and test or reset status flags may or may not be passed on to the programmer (see Chapter 9). However, users do not need to trap exceptions. It is common practice to rely on the standard responses described in Table 7.1, assuming the interpreter or compiler in use masks the exceptions as its default action.

The appearance of a NaN in the output of a program is a sure sign that something has gone wrong. The appearance of ∞ in the output may or may not indicate a programming error, depending on the context. When writing programs where division by zero is a possibility, the programmer should be cautious. Operations with ∞ should not be used unless a careful analysis has ensured that they are appropriate.

The IEEE Philosophy on Exceptions

The IEEE approach to exceptions permits a very efficient and reliable approach to programming in general, which may be summarized as: *Try the easy fast way first; fix it later if an exception occurs.* For example, suppose it is desired to compute

$$\sqrt{x^2 + y^2}. \tag{7.3}$$

Even if the result is within the normalized range of the floating point system, a direct implementation might result in overflow. The traditional careful implementation would guard against overflow by scaling x and y by $\max(|x|, |y|)$ before squaring. But with IEEE arithmetic, the direct computation may be used. The idea is to first clear the exception status flags, then do the computation, and then check the status flags. In the unlikely event that overflow (or underflow) has occured, the program can take the necessary action. For details of how to compute (7.3) in Fortran 2003, for example, see [MRC04, Section 11.10.4]. For a more extensive discussion of how this idea can be used for many different numerical computations, see [DL94]. To make such ideas practical, it is essential that the IEEE standard be properly supported by both software and hardware, so that setting and testing the status exception flags is permitted by the programming language in use, and does not significantly slow down execution of the program.

Hardware support for the standard for a specific class of machines is discussed in the next chapter, and software support is discussed in the following chapter. Although support for the standard is still far from perfect, it has steadily improved over the years. For some more thoughts on these issues, as well as some interesting comments on alternative arithmetic models, see [Dem91].

Chapter 8

The Intel Microprocessors

The two largest manufacturers of the microprocessor chips that were used in the early personal computers incorporated the IEEE standard in their design; these were Intel (whose chips were used by IBM PCs and clones) and Motorola (whose 68000 series chips were used by the Apple Macintosh II and the early Sun workstations). Later microprocessors, such as the Sun Sparc, DEC Alpha, and IBM RS/6000 and Power PC, also followed the standard. Even the IBM 390, the successor to the 360/370 series, offers support for the IEEE standard as an alternative to the long-supported hexadecimal format. We shall confine our attention to the Intel microprocessors, since these chips were and still are the most widely used. The total number of individual computers using these chips is conservatively estimated to be in the hundreds of millions.

The original Intel microprocessor was the 8086 chip, announced in 1978. This chip included a central processing unit (CPU) and an arithmetic-logical unit (ALU) but did not support floating point operations. In 1980, Intel announced the 8087 and 8088 chips, which were used in the first IBM PCs. The 8088 was a modification of the 8086. The 8087 was the floating point coprocessor, providing a floating point unit (FPU) on a separate chip from the 8088. The 8087 was revolutionary in a number of respects. It was unprecedented that so much functionality could be provided by such a small chip. Many of the features of the IEEE standard were first implemented on the 8087. The extended format recommended by the standard was based on the 8087 design.

The successors of the 8087, the 80287 and 80387, were also coprocessors, implemented separately from the main chip. However, later microprocessors in the series, namely the 80486 DX, the Pentium, the Pentium Pro, the Pentium II, and the Pentium III, included the FPU on the main chip. Though each machine was faster than its predecessor, the architecture of the Pentium FPUs remained essentially the same as that of the 8087. We will now describe this in some detail.

Hardware Extended Precision

Floating point instructions operate primarily on data stored in eight 80-bit floating point registers, each of which can accommodate an extended format floating point number (see Chapter 4). However, it was expected that programs would usually store variables in memory using the single or double format. The extended precision registers were provided with the idea that a sequence of floating point instructions, operating on data in registers, would produce an accumulated result that is more accurate than if the computations were done using only single or double precision. This more accurate accumulated result would then be rounded to fit the single or double format and stored to memory when the sequence of computations is completed, perhaps giving the correctly rounded value of the exact result, which would be unlikely to happen when a sequence of operations uses the same precision as the final result. Although the IEEE standard encourages this practice, it also requires that the user have the option of disabling it through use of a *precision mode*.[15] The precision mode may be set to any of the supported formats; for example, if the precision mode in effect is *single*, the floating point computations must deliver results that are rounded to single precision before being stored in the extended format register. A subtle point is that even if the precision mode in effect is *single*, a floating point value that overflows the single format does not generate an exception, as long as it does not overflow the extended format.

The Register Stack

Another interesting feature is the organization of the floating point registers in a logical stack. The eight registers are numbered 0 to 7. At any given time, the top register in the stack is denoted by ST(0), the second-to-top register ST(1), etc. The actual physical register corresponding to the top register ST(0) is determined by a top-of-stack pointer stored in a 3-bit field of the 16-bit *status word*, which is stored in a dedicated 16-bit register. If this bitstring is 011, for example, ST(0) is equivalent to physical register 3, ST(1) is equivalent to physical register 4, and so on; thus, ST(7) is physical register 2. When the register stack is *pushed*, the top-of-stack pointer is *decremented*; e.g., the top register is changed from physical register 3 to physical register 2, ST(1) becomes physical register 3, and ST(7) becomes physical register 1.

The register stack is very convenient for the evaluation of arithmetic expressions. For example, consider the task of computing the expression

$$(a + b) \times c,$$

assuming the floating point numbers a, b, and c are available in memory locations A, B, and C, respectively, and that the result is to be stored in memory location X. A sequence of assembly language instructions that will carry out this task is

```
FLD    A
FLD    B
FADD
FLD    C
FMUL
FSTP   X
```

Here the first FLD instruction *pushes* the value in memory location A onto the stack; in other words, it first decrements the top-of-stack pointer and then copies the value in A, namely a, to the new stack register ST(0). The second FLD instruction then pushes the value in the memory location B onto the stack; this requires decrementing the stack pointer and copying the value in B, namely b, to the new ST(0). At this point ST(0) contains b and ST(1) contains a. The FADD instruction then *adds* the value in ST(0) to the value in ST(1) and *pops* the stack, i.e., increments the top-of-stack pointer. The third FLD instruction pushes the value in location C, namely c, onto the stack. Then the FMUL instruction multiplies the new value in ST(0), namely c, onto the value in ST(1), namely $a + b$, and pops the stack, leaving the final value of the expression in the top register ST(0). Finally, the FSTP instruction stores the final result in memory location X, popping the stack one more time. The register stack now

---

[15]Called rounding precision mode in the standard.

Table 8.1: Logical Register Stack Contents, at Successive Times

Register	Time 0	Time 1	Time 2	Time 3	Time 4	Time 5
ST(0)		a	b	$a \oplus b$	c	$(a \oplus b) \otimes c$
ST(1)			a		$a \oplus b$	
ST(2)						
ST(3)						
ST(4)						
ST(5)						
ST(6)						
ST(7)						

Table 8.2: Physical Register Stack Contents, at Successive Times

Register	Time 0	Time 1	Time 2	Time 3	Time 4	Time 5
P.R. 0						
P.R. 1			$\rightarrow b$	b	$\rightarrow c$	c
P.R. 2		$\rightarrow a$	a	$\rightarrow a \oplus b$	$a \oplus b$	$\rightarrow (a \oplus b) \otimes c$
P.R. 3	$\rightarrow$					
P.R. 4						
P.R. 5						
P.R. 6						
P.R. 7						

has the same configuration that it did before the expression evaluation began (either empty or containing some other results still to be processed). The whole computation is summarized in Table 8.1.

Note that the computation is always organized so that the latest result is at the top of the stack. The values in the registers are floating point numbers, not formulas. The expression $a \oplus b$ is used rather than $a + b$, because this is the actual computed value, the rounded value of $a + b$.

Suppose ST(0) is initially equivalent to physical register 3. Then the contents of the physical registers during the expression evaluation are shown in Table 8.2. The symbol $\rightarrow$ indicates the top register in the stack at each point in time.

Each time the register stack is pushed, the top register, ST(0), moves one position in terms of the physical registers. Also, when the register stack is popped and ST(0) moves back to its previous position, the numerical value in the physical register remains unchanged until it is overwritten, e.g., by a subsequent push instruction.

The register stack can handle arithmetic expressions nested up to seven levels. However, it is possible to overflow the stack by pushing it too many times. When this happens, an invalid operation is signaled and the standard response is to return a NaN. Consequently, compiler writers need to bear this in mind so that stack overflow does not occur when complicated expressions are parsed. The original idea was to handle stack overflows, which could be expected to be rare, through interrupt software, to give compiler writers the illusion of an unlimited stack. Although this idea was promoted enthusiastically by Kahan, it was never implemented [PH97, p. 319].

There are other versions of the floating point arithmetic instructions that require only one operand to be in a register and the other operand to be in memory. Though these result in shorter assembly language programs, they make the functionality of the stack somewhat less clear.

Exercise 8.1 *Give a sequence of assembly language instructions to compute*

$$a + (b \times c)$$

and show, by modifying Tables 8.1 and 8.2, how the computation progresses.

Exercise 8.2 *Give a floating point expression whose evaluation would overflow the register stack.*

Status Flags, Exception Masks, Rounding and Precision Modes

In addition to the top-of-stack pointer, the *status word* also contains the five exception status flags that are required by the IEEE standard. A flag is set to 1 when the corresponding exception takes place. These flags can be cleared by special assembly language instructions such as FCLEX.

Besides the status word, the floating point unit has another special word called the *control word*, which is stored in another dedicated 16-bit register. The control word is used to set the *rounding mode*, the *precision mode*, and the *exception masks*. Four bits of the control word (two bits for each mode) are used to encode the rounding mode (see Chapter 5) and the precision mode (see the discussion at the beginning of this chapter). Five bits in the control word are reserved for exception masks.[16] When an exception occurs and the corresponding flag in the status word is set, the corresponding mask in the control word is examined. If the exception mask is 0, the exception is trapped and control is passed to a user-provided trapping routine. If the exception mask is 1, i.e., the exception is masked, the processor takes the default action described in Table 7.1 and execution continues normally.

The floating point environment is set to a default initial state by the assembly language instruction FNINIT. This clears all status flags in the status word, and sets the control word as follows: the rounding mode is *round to nearest*, the precision mode is *extended*, and all exceptions are masked. Other instructions are provided to set the rounding mode, precision mode, or exception masks in the control word to desired values.

The Itanium Chip and Fused Multiply-Add

In 2000, Intel announced its new IA 64 Itanium chip. The Itanium complies with the IEEE standard, and its floating point registers support the same 80-bit extended format as the 8087 and Pentium. However, the Itanium architecture departs radically from that of Intel's previous microprocessors. Most significant, as far as floating point is concerned, is the fact that it has 128 floating point registers, compared with 8 on the Pentium. Another significant change is that the Itanium includes a *fused multiply-add instruction* (FMA). The FMA computes the correctly rounded value

$$\text{round}(a \times b + c), \tag{8.1}$$

---

[16]The status and control words also respectively store a status flag and corresponding exception mask not required by the IEEE standard. This additional status flag is set when an operation with a subnormal operand takes place.

CHAPTER 8. THE INTEL MICROPROCESSORS

which is generally a more accurate approximation to the exact result than computing

$$\text{round}(\text{round}(a \times b) + c). \tag{8.2}$$

The FMA instruction is very useful because many floating point programs include the operation $a \times b + c$ in their inner loops. The FMA was developed earlier by IBM as part of its RS/6000 architecture and is used by its descendant, the Power PC. Support for the FMA instruction is not discussed by the IEEE standard but is addressed in its ongoing revision [IEE-R]. Kahan [Kah97] describes the FMA as a "mixed blessing," with some disadvantages as well as obvious advantages.

Exercise 8.3 *Find single format floating point numbers a, b, and c for which (8.1) and (8.2) are different, assuming the destination format for each operation is IEEE single.*

Chapter 9

Programming Languages

Programs for the first stored program electronic computers consisted of a list of machine instructions coded in binary. It was a considerable advance when assemblers became available, so that a programmer could use mnemonic codes such as LOAD X, instead of needing to know the code for the instruction to load a variable from memory to a register and the physical address of the memory location. The first widely available higher level programming language was developed at IBM in the mid 1950s and called Fortran, for formula translation. Programmers could write instructions such as x = (a + b)*c, and the compiler would then determine the necessary machine language instructions to be executed. Fortran became extremely popular and is still widely used for scientific computing today. Soon after Fortran was established, the programming language ALGOL was developed by an international group of academic computer scientists. Although ALGOL had many nicer programming constructs than Fortran, it never achieved the latter's success, mainly because Fortran was designed to be highly efficient from its inception, which ALGOL was not.[16] However, many of the innovations of ALGOL, such as the notions of block structure and recursion, survived in subsequent programming languages, including Pascal, which appeared in the 1970s. These notions also greatly influenced later modifications of Fortran, particularly the major revisions Fortran 77 and Fortran 90 in 1977 and 1990, respectively.

In the 1980s, the programming language C, a product of Bell Labs, emerged as the *lingua franca* of computing. C was used as the foundation of the object-oriented language C++, which in turn led to Java, the language developed by Sun in the 1990s. Fortran remains very popular for numerical computing because of the availability of fast optimizing compilers on all machines, as well as the existence of billions of lines of legacy code. However, C and C++ are also widely used for numerical computing, and Java is being promoted as an alternative with much promise because of its portable binary code and its emphasis on reliability.

Netlib [Net] is a valuable resource for free numerical software to solve all kinds of problems. For example, LAPACK (Linear Algebra package) is a state-of-the-art package for solving problems from linear algebra. LAPACK is portable software, built on the BLAS (Basic Linear Algebra Subroutines), which are fine-tuned for high performance on specific machines. Most of Netlib's programs are written in Fortran, but C, C++, and Java packages are also available.

---

[16]Wilkes writes [Wil98], "As an intellectual achievement, Fortran was stillborn by its very success as a practical tool."

Language Support for IEEE 754

The record of language support for the IEEE floating point standard is mixed. To make good use of hardware that supports the standard, a programming language should define types that are compatible with the IEEE formats, allow control of the rounding mode (and the precision mode when it exists), provide the standard responses to exceptions as the default behavior, allow access to and resetting of the exception status flags, and allow trapping of exceptions. All of these were provided soon after the publication of IEEE 754 by Apple in SANE (Standard Apple Numerics Environment) [App88], using the Pascal and C languages. Unfortunately, in the words of Kahan, "Apple never received the accolade it deserved from the marketplace" [Kah97], and its fine example was not followed by many others, although SANE did evolve into a similar support system for Apple's Power PC Macintosh. The Fortran and C language international standards committees have, until recently, shied away from support for IEEE 754. The result has been that the standardized hardware features have not been generally available to users programming in higher level languages. Furthermore, in cases where support is provided, different vendors have provided different mechanisms for access. In brief, software support for IEEE 754 since publication of the standard has been as inconsistent as was hardware support for floating point during the previous three decades.

C99 and Fortran 2003

Thanks to the efforts of the ANSI Fortran committee X3J3 and the Numerical C Extensions Group (NCEG), the situation has finally improved. An International Standards Organization/International Electrotechnical Commission (ISO/IEC) revision of the Fortran standard, known as Fortran 2003, was recently approved, and the long-awaited ISO/IEC revision of the C language standard, known as C99, was completed in December 1999 [ISO99]. Although neither Fortran 2003 nor C99 require every implementation to support IEEE 754, they both provide standardized mechanisms for accessing its features when supported by the hardware. For information on Fortran 2003, see [MRC04]. C99 introduces a macro,[17] `__STDC_IEC_559__`, which is supposed to be predefined by implementations supporting IEEE 754. Any implementation defining this macro must then conform with various requirements. The types *float* and *double* must use the IEEE single and double formats, respectively, and it is recommended that type *long double* fit the IEEE extended format requirements. The implementation must provide access to status flags such as `FE_DIVBYZERO`, control of rounding modes via macros such as `FE_DOWNWARD`, and access to special constants via macros such as `INFINITY`. Other macros with function syntax must also be provided, such as `isnan` to determine if a number has a NaN value, and `isnormal` to test if a value is in the normalized range. Details are given in Annex F of [ISO99]. In the next chapter, we discuss how to write simple numerical programs in C, but we do not attempt to illustrate the use of the macros.

Java

The situation with Java is quite different. The Java language types *float* and *double* are required to conform to the IEEE single and double floating point formats. Unfortunately, the well-publicized requirements of the Java language and the IEEE floating point standard have major conflicts with each other. For example, Java insists that the results of arithmetic operations be rounded to nearest, in contradiction to the IEEE

---

[17] As mentioned earlier, the international name of IEEE 754 is IEC 559.

CHAPTER 9. PROGRAMMING LANGUAGES

requirement that four rounding modes be supported. Another major difficulty is that Java programs are required to give identical output on all platforms, while the IEEE floating point standard specifically allows, but does not require, extended precision computation for intermediate results that are later to be rounded to narrower formats (see Chapter 8). The fact that Sun and Intel have opposite positions on this matter does not bode well for a quick resolution. However, some progress has been made. Java 1.2 relaxed the requirement somewhat to allow use of the precision mode discussed in Chapter 8 to disable extended precision. This permits the inconsistency that on a Sun Sparc, for example, a double precision computation might result in overflow, while on an Intel Pentium, if an intermediate part of the same computation is performed using the extended precision registers with the precision mode set to double, overflow might not occur (see Chapter 8). See [Kah98] for the case against disabling extended precision, and see [Jav] for current developments in numerical aspects of Java.

In fact, complete programming language support for the IEEE standard involves much more than the main issues mentioned above. For more detailed discussions, see [Dar98, Fig00, Gol91].

MATLAB

The interactive system MATLAB offers a very attractive alternative to conventional compiled languages. MATLAB is extremely popular because of its ease of use, its convenient and accurate matrix operations, its extensive software toolboxes, and its graphics capabilities. Furthermore, although MATLAB is normally used in interpreted mode, it is possible to compile MATLAB code for increased efficiency, as well as to call C, Fortran, and Java subprograms. MATLAB uses IEEE arithmetic with the double format, with exceptions masked so that the standard responses take place (see Table 7.1). However, MATLAB does not provide access to control of rounding and precision or to the exception status flags.[18] We highly recommend MATLAB, but we do not discuss it here, because many books on the subject are available; see especially [HH00]. The plots in Chapters 11 and 12 were produced using MATLAB.

Complex Arithmetic

Fortran and C99 support data types for complex numbers. In MATLAB, every variable is (potentially) complex. Complex arithmetic is implemented in software, calling on the hardware to carry out the necessary real arithmetic operations. Thus, for example, taking the square root of a complex variable with a negative real part and a zero imaginary part yields a complex result with a zero real part and a nonzero imaginary part, not a NaN, since the hardware square root operation generated by the compiler or interpreter has a positive real argument (the complex modulus).

Floating point computation is an option in symbolic computing systems such as *Maple* and *Mathematica*. It is also used in other familiar software, such as spreadsheet programs.

---

[18]There is an exception: on an Intel machine running MATLAB 6, it is possible to change the rounding and precision modes. To change the rounding mode, type `system_dependent('setround',r)`, where r is one of Inf (for *round up*), −Inf (for *round down*), 0 (for *round towards zero*), or 'nearest' (or 0.5) (for *round to nearest*, the default). To change the precision mode, type `system_dependent('setprecision',p)`, where p is one of 64 (for *extended*), 53 (for *double*, the default), or 24 (for *single*) (see Table 4.4).

Chapter 10

Floating Point in C

The C programming language became very popular in the 1980s. A good reference for the language is [Rob95]. Here we discuss how to get started with floating point computation in C.

Float and Double, Input and Output

In C, the type *float* normally refers to the IEEE floating point single format, and when we do computations with variables of type *float*, we say we are using single precision. Here is an echo program that reads in a floating point number using the standard input routine `scanf` and prints it out again using the standard output routine `printf`:

```
main ()      /*  Program 1: Echo  */
{
   float x;
   scanf("%f", &x);
   printf("x = %f", x);
}
```

The second argument to the `scanf` statement is not the *value* of the variable x but the *address* of x; this is the meaning of the & symbol. The address is required because the input routine needs to know where to store the value that is read. On the other hand, the second argument to the `printf` statement is the *value* of the variable x. The first argument to both routines is a *control string*. The two standard *format codes* used for specifying floating point numbers in these control strings are %f and %e. These refer, respectively, to *fixed decimal* and *exponential decimal* formats. Actually, %f and %e have identical effects when used with the input routine `scanf`, which can process input in either a fixed decimal format (e.g., 0.666) or an exponential decimal format (e.g., 6.66e-1, meaning 6.66×10^{-1}). However, different format codes have different effects when used with the output routine `printf`. The `scanf` routine calls a decimal to binary conversion routine to convert the input decimal format to the internal binary floating point representation, and the `printf` routine calls a binary to decimal conversion routine to convert the floating point representation to the output decimal format. The C99 standard recommends that both conversion routines use the rounding mode that is in effect to correctly round the results.

Assuming Program 1 has been saved in a file and compiled, let us consider the output when it is executed. Table 10.1 shows the output of Program 1 for various output formats in the `printf` statement, when the input is 0.66666663666666666666 (the value of 2/3 to 20 digits).

Table 10.1: Output of Program 1 for Various Output Format Codes

Format code	Output
%f	0.666667
%e	6.666667e-01
%8.3f	0.667
%8.3e	6.667e-01
%21.15f	0.666666686534882
%21.15e	6.666666865348816e-01

The %f format code generates output in a fixed decimal output, while %e generates exponential notation. Neither of them echoes the input to the accuracy given originally, since it is not possible to store the value of 2/3 to 20 accurate digits using single precision. Instead, the input value is correctly rounded to 24 bits of precision in its significand, which, as we saw earlier, corresponds to approximately 7 significant decimal digits. Consequently, the format codes %f and %e print, by default, 6 digits after the decimal point, but %e shows a little more accuracy than %f since the digit before the decimal point is nonzero. In both cases, the decimal output is rounded, using the default *round to nearest* mode; this explains the final digit 7. The next two lines of the table show how to print the number to *less* precision if so desired. The 8 refers to the total field width, and the 3 to the number of digits after the decimal point. The last two lines show an attempt to print the number to *more* precision, but we see that about half the digits have no significance. The output is the result of converting the single precision binary representation of 2/3 to more than the 7 decimal digits to which it agrees with the value that was input. The output would be exactly the same if, instead of reading the value 0.66666666666666666666 for x, we set the value of x equal to the quotient 2.0/3.0. It is important to realize that regardless of the decimal output format, the floating point variables are *always* stored using the IEEE binary formats described in Chapter 4.

Using the %f format code is not a good idea unless it is known that the numbers are neither too small nor too large. For example, if Program 1 is run on the input 1.0e-10, the output using %f is 0.000000, since it is not possible to print the desired value more accurately using only 6 digits after the decimal point without using exponential notation. Using %e we get the desired result 1.000000e-10. A useful alternative is %g, which chooses either a fixed or an exponential display, whichever is shorter.

We can represent the value of 2/3 more accurately by declaring x to have type *double* instead of *float*. Type *double* uses the IEEE floating point double format,[19] and when we do computations with variables of type *double*, we say we are using double precision. But if we change *float* to *double* in Program 1, we get a completely wrong answer such as -6.392091e-236 (using the %e output format code). The problem here is that the %f in the input format code instructs the scanf routine to store the input value in the IEEE single format at the address given by &x; scanf does not know the type of x, only its address. When x is printed, its value is converted to decimal assuming it is stored in the double format. Therefore, any scanf statement that reads a double variable must use the control format code %lf or %le (for long float or long exponential) instead of %f or %e, so that the result is stored in the IEEE double format. Do not attempt to use %d to refer to the double format; %d actually

---

[19]The name *long float* was used in the past but is obsolete in this context.

means integer format.

The `printf` control string does *not* need to use `%lf` or `%le` (as opposed to `%f` or `%e`) when printing the values of *double* variables. This is because `printf` *always* expects *double* variables, and so *float* variables are always automatically converted to *double* values before being passed to the output routine. Therefore, since `printf` always receives *double* arguments, it treats the control strings `%e` and `%le` exactly the same; likewise `%f` and `%lf`, `%g` and `%lg`. However, the default, if no field width and precision are specified, is to output the number to approximately the precision of the single format, so we need to specify higher precision output to see more digits. In summary, then, if we change *float* to *double* in the variable declaration, change `%f` to `%lf` in the `scanf` statement, and change `%e` to `%21.15e` in the `printf` statement, we obtain an output that has 15 significant digits after the decimal point.

Choice of the wrong output format code can have serious implications! A good example is the story of a German state election in 1992. According to the rules of this election, a minimum of 5% of the vote was required for a party to be allocated any seats in the parliament. The evening of the election, results were announced declaring that the Green party had received exactly 5% of the vote. After midnight it was discovered that the Greens actually had only 4.97% of the vote. The program that printed out the percentages showed only one place after the decimal, and had rounded the count up to 5% [WW92].

Exercise 10.1 *Supposing that the German election program was written in C, what output format code would have led to the incorrect conclusion that the Greens had exactly 5% of the vote? What would have been a better output format code?*

Exercise 10.2 *(D. Gay) The wrong answer obtained by Program 1 if* float *is changed to* double *without any change to the* scanf *format depends on whether the machine uses Big Endian or Little Endian addressing (see the end of Chapter 4). Why is this? If you have machines of both kinds available, experiment to see what results you obtain on each.*

Two Loop Programs

Let us now consider a program with a "while loop":

```
main()    /* Program 2: First Loop Program */
{
   int n = 0;
   float x = 1;

/* Repeatedly divide x by 2 until it underflows to 0 */

   while (x > 0) {
      x = x/2;
      n++;
      printf("(2 raised to the power -%d) = %e \n", n, x);
   }
}
```

Program 2 initializes an IEEE single format floating point variable x to 1, and then repeatedly divides it by 2. We could, for clarity, replace 2 in the statement x = x/2 by 2.0, but this is not necessary because x has type *float*. (If x had type *int*, the integer division operator would be used instead, giving the result 0, for example, if x had the value 1.) The termination test is x > 0: the loop continues to execute as long as x is positive, but terminates when x is zero (or negative). The statement n++ increments the integer n by 1 during every pass through the loop, keeping track of how many times it is executed. (This statement is shorthand for n = n + 1.) The printf statement displays the values of n and x, which by construction satisfy the equation

$$x = 2^{-n}$$

as long as the arithmetic is done exactly. The \n is the *newline* character, needed so that the output is displayed one line at a time. If the arithmetic were to be done exactly, Program 2 would run forever, but in floating point, the value of the variable x will underflow to zero eventually. What is the output using IEEE arithmetic?[20]

Here is the answer:

```
(2 raised to the power -1) = 5.000000e-01
(2 raised to the power -2) = 2.500000e-01
(2 raised to the power -3) = 1.250000e-01
(2 raised to the power -4) = 6.250000e-02
(2 raised to the power -5) = 3.125000e-02

    .... 140 lines omitted ....

(2 raised to the power -146) = 1.121039e-44
(2 raised to the power -147) = 5.605194e-45
(2 raised to the power -148) = 2.802597e-45
(2 raised to the power -149) = 1.401298e-45
(2 raised to the power -150) = 0.000000e+00
```

Here is the explanation. The variable x is reduced from its initial value of 1 to 1/2, 1/4, 1/8, etc. After the first 126 times through the loop, x has been reduced to the smallest IEEE single normalized number, $N_{\min} = 2^{-126}$. If there were no subnormal numbers, x would underflow to zero after one more step through the loop. Instead, gradual underflow requires that the next step reduce x to the subnormal number 2^{-127}, which has the representation

| 0 | 00000000 | 10000000000000000000000 |

The next step reduces x to 2^{-128}, with the representation

| 0 | 00000000 | 01000000000000000000000 |

This continues 21 more times, until x reaches 2^{-149}, with the representation

| 0 | 00000000 | 00000000000000000000001 |

After one more step, we would like x to have the value 2^{-150}, but this is not representable in the IEEE single format. We have a choice of rounding it up to 2^{-149} or down to 0. In either case, we make an absolute rounding error of 2^{-150}. The default rounding mode, round to nearest, chooses the one with the 0 final bit, namely, the number 0.

---

[20]Some machines support gradual underflow only in software. On such machines, the compiler's default option may *not* be to support IEEE arithmetic. Some machines provide compiler options to specify that IEEE arithmetic is to be used, but some do not.

CHAPTER 10. FLOATING POINT IN C

Now let us consider a different loop program:

```
main()    /* Program 3: Second Loop Program */
{
   int n = 0;
   float x = 1, y = 2;

/* Repeatedly divide x by 2 until y = (1 + x) rounds to 1 */

   while (y > 1) {
      x = x/2;
      y = 1 + x;
      n++;
      printf("1 added to (2 raised to the power -%d) = %e \n', n, y);
   }
}
```

In Program 3, the variable x (with type *float*) is again initialized to 1 and repeatedly divided by 2, but this time the termination test is different: the loop continues as long as y is greater than 1, where y is set to the value of $1 + x$, but terminates if the value of y is exactly 1 (or smaller). What is the output using IEEE arithmetic?

Here is the answer:

```
1 added to (2 raised to the power -1) = 1.500000e+00
1 added to (2 raised to the power -2) = 1.250000e+00
1 added to (2 raised to the power -3) = 1.125000e+00
1 added to (2 raised to the power -4) = 1.062500e+00
1 added to (2 raised to the power -5) = 1.031250e+00

         .... 10 lines omitted ....

1 added to (2 raised to the power -16) = 1.000015e+00
1 added to (2 raised to the power -17) = 1.000008e+00
1 added to (2 raised to the power -18) = 1.000004e+00
1 added to (2 raised to the power -19) = 1.000002e+00
1 added to (2 raised to the power -20) = 1.000001e+00
1 added to (2 raised to the power -21) = 1.000000e+00
1 added to (2 raised to the power -22) = 1.000000e+00
1 added to (2 raised to the power -23) = 1.000000e+00
1 added to (2 raised to the power -24) = 1.000000e+00
```

Program 3 terminates much sooner than Program 2 does. Recall that $1 + 2^{-23}$ has the exact representation

| 0 | 01111111 | 00000000000000000000001 |

However, even though the number 2^{-24} can be represented exactly using the IEEE single format, the number $1 + 2^{-24}$ cannot. We have a choice of rounding it up to $1 + 2^{-23}$ or down to 1. As earlier, both choices are equally close, this time with an absolute rounding error of 2^{-24}. Again, the default rounding mode, round to nearest, chooses the answer with the zero final bit, namely, the number 1. Consequently, the loop terminates.

At first sight, it seems from the output that the loop should have terminated earlier, when x reached the value 2^{-21}. However, this is because the output format code `%e` used in the `printf` statement does not display enough decimal digits. Six digits after the decimal point are not quite enough. We can insist on seeing seven by changing the `printf` statement to

```
printf("1 added to (2 raised to the power -%d) = %.7e \n", n, y);
```

in which case the last few lines of output become

```
1 added to (2 raised to the power -20) = 1.0000010e+00
1 added to (2 raised to the power -21) = 1.0000005e+00
1 added to (2 raised to the power -22) = 1.0000002e+00
1 added to (2 raised to the power -23) = 1.0000001e+00
1 added to (2 raised to the power -24) = 1.0000000e+00
```

We could have coded Program 3 without using the variable `y`, replacing it by `1 + x` in both the while loop termination test and the `printf` statement. However, when we do this, we are no longer sure that the value of `1 + x` will be rounded to the IEEE single format. Indeed, on an Intel machine, e.g., a Pentium, the value of `1 + x` would then likely be held in an extended 80-bit register. If so, the program would run through the loop more times before it terminates.

Exercise 10.3 *Write a C program to store the value of $1/10$ in a float variable and then repeatedly divide the number by 2 until it is subnormal. Continue dividing by 2 until about half the precision of the number is lost. Then reverse the process, multiplying by 2 the same number of times you divided by 2. Display the final result. How many significant digits does it have? Explain why this happened.*

Exercise 10.4 *What would happen if Programs 2 and 3 were executed using the rounding mode round up? Make a prediction and then, if your C compiler supports the rounding modes, do the experiment.*

Exercise 10.5 *Recalling Exercise 6.12, write a C program to find the smallest positive integer x such that the floating point expression*

$$(1 \oslash x) \otimes x$$

is not 1, using single precision. Make sure that the variable `x` *has type* float, *and assign the value of the expression $1 \oslash x$ to a* float *variable before doing the multiplication operation, to prevent the use of extended precision or an optimization by the compiler from defeating your experiment. Repeat with double precision.*

Exercise 10.6 *Again recalling Exercise 6.12, write a C program to find the smallest positive integer x such that*

$$1 \oslash (1 \oslash x)$$

is not x, using single precision. Repeat with double precision. (See the comments in the previous exercise.)

Table 10.2: Parallel Resistance Results

R_1	R_2	Total resistance
1	1	5.000000e-01
1	10	9.090909e-01
1	1000	9.990010e-01
1	1.0e5	9.999900e-01
1	1.0e10	1.000000e+00
1	0.1	9.090909e-02
1	1.0e-5	9.999900e-06
1	1.0e-10	1.000000e-10
1	0	0.000000e+00

Infinity and Division by Zero

Now let us turn our attention to exceptions. Program 4 implements the parallel resistance formula (7.1):

```
main() /* Program 4: Parallel Resistance Formula */
{
   float r1,r2, total;

   printf("Enter the two resistances \n");
   scanf("%f %f", &r1, &r2);  /* input the resistances of the two
                                 resistors connected in parallel */
   printf("r1 = %e   r2 = %e \n", r1, r2);
   total=1 / (1/r1 + 1/r2); /* formula for total resistance */
   printf("Total resistance is %e \n",total);
}
```

Table 10.2 summarizes the output of Program 4 for various input data. In the first five lines, R_1 is held fixed equal to 1 and R_2 is increased from 1 to a large number. The larger R_2 is, the more the current tends to flow through the first resistor, and so the closer the total resistance is to 1. With R_1 fixed equal to 1, and R_2 sufficiently large, i.e., $1/R_2$ sufficiently small, the floating point sum of $1/R_2$ and $1/R_1$ is precisely 1 even though the exact result would be strictly greater than 1 for all finite nonnegative values of R_2. Thus, the final result (the inverse of the sum) is precisely 1, even though the mathematical result is strictly less than 1. This is, of course, because of the limited precision of an IEEE single format floating point number.

The last four lines of the table show what happens when R_1 is fixed equal to 1 and R_2 is decreased below 1. The smaller R_2 is, the more the current tends to flow through the second resistor.

The last line of the table shows that the output zero is obtained when $R_2 = 0$; as explained in Chapter 7, this is a sensible mathematical result. This result is obtained only if the floating point environment is set properly, so that the standard response to division by zero takes place, i.e., so that the result of the quotient $1/0$ is set to ∞. This is the default on most systems.

Exercise 10.7 *If $R_1 = 1$, for approximately what range of values for R_2 (what powers of 10) does Program 4 give a result exactly equal to 1? Try to work out the answer before you run the program.*

Table 10.3: Some Standard C Math Library Functions

fabs	absolute value: `fabs(x)` returns $\|x\|$
sqrt	square root: `sqrt(x)` returns $\sqrt{x}$
exp	exponential (base e): `exp(x)` returns e^x
log	logarithm (base e): `log(x)` returns $\log_e(x)$
log10	logarithm (base 10): `log10(x)` returns $\log_{10}(x)$
sin	sine (argument given in radians)
cos	cosine (argument given in radians)
atan	arctangent (result in radians between $-\pi/2$ and $\pi/2$)
pow	power (two arguments: `pow(x,y)` returns x^y)

Exercise 10.8 *How does the answer to Exercise 10.7 change if $R_1 = 1000$: approximately what range of values for R_2 give a result exactly equal to 1000? Explain your reasoning.*

Exercise 10.9 *How does the answer to Exercise 10.7 change if the rounding mode is changed to* round up*? If your compiler supports the rounding modes, try the experiment.*

The Math Library

Very often, numerical programs need to evaluate standard mathematical functions. The *exponential* function is defined by

$$\exp(x) = e^x = \lim_{n \to \infty} \left(1 + \frac{x}{n}\right)^n. \tag{10.1}$$

It maps the extended real line (including $\pm\infty$) to the nonnegative extended real numbers, with the convention that $\exp(-\infty) = 0$ and $\exp(\infty) = \infty$. Its inverse is the *logarithmic* function (base e), $\log(x)$, satisfying

$$\exp(x) = y \quad \text{if and only if} \quad x = \log(y).$$

The function $\log(y)$ is defined for $y \geq 0$ with the conventions that $\log(0) = -\infty$ and $\log(\infty) = \infty$. These functions, along with many others such as the trigonometric functions, are provided by all C compilers as part of an associated *math library*. Some of them are listed in Table 10.3. They all expect *double* arguments and return *double* values, but they can be called with *float* arguments and their values assigned to *float* variables; the conversions are done automatically. The C99 standard calls for the support of variants such as `expf` and `expl`, which expect and return *float* and *long double* types, respectively, but these are rarely needed. The C99 standard also calls for support for other mathematical functions not traditionally provided, including `fma`, the fused multiply-add operation (with a single rounding error) described at the end of Chapter 8.

Neither the IEEE standard nor the C99 standard prescribe the accuracy of the irrational-valued math library functions (with the exception of the square root function). The library functions can usually be presumed to deliver approximately correctly rounded results; i.e., given a floating point argument x, return a function value that agrees with the true function value $f(x)$ to within about an ulp; however, this may not always be the case [Kah96a]. One of the motivations for the provision of extended precision by the IEEE standard was to allow fast accurate computation of the library functions [Hou81]. There is a fundamental difficulty in computing correctly rounded values of the exponential, logarithmic, and trigonometric functions, called the Tablemaker's Dilemma: one might have to compute an arbitrarily large number of correct digits before one would know whether to round the result up or down. However, clever algorithms can nonetheless achieve correctly rounded results by using sufficiently high precision when necessary [Mul97].

More importantly, if x is not a floating point number and so must first be rounded before f is evaluated, the library functions do *not* necessarily return a value that agrees with $f(x)$ within about an ulp. This phenomenon is discussed in Chapter 12.

C99 calls for the math library functions to return infinite or NaN values when appropriate. For example, log returns $-\infty$ when its argument is 0 and NaN when its argument is negative. The case where the argument is -0 is controversial. Kahan argues that the math library functions should return results that distinguish the sign of 0, so that, e.g., $\log(-0)$ returns NaN. One motivation for this is that one may think of -0 as representing a negative underflowed quantity; a compelling application is the use of branch cuts to define complex-valued functions [Gol91, Kah97]. However, the C99 standard says that $\log(-0)$ must return the same value as $\log(0)$, i.e., $-\infty$.

When a C program contains calls to the math library, it should have the following line at the start of the program:

```
#include <math.h>
```

The "include file" `math.h` tells the C compiler about the return types and other calling-sequence details of the functions provided in the math library. Also, when the program is compiled, it is necessary to *link* the math library; the syntax for this is system-dependent. If an error message says that the math functions cannot be found, the math library is not properly linked.

Exercise 10.10 *Check to see what your C math library returns for* $\log(\pm 0)$, $\log(\pm 1)$, *and* $\log(\pm\infty)$. *The result may depend on whether your compiler supports C99.*

Exercise 10.11 *The domain of a function is the set of values on which it is defined, and its range is the set of all possible values that it returns.*

1. *What are the ranges of the* sin *and* cos *functions?*

2. *What values should* $\sin(\infty)$ *and* $\cos(\infty)$ *return? Check to see if your C math library does what you expect. The results may depend on whether your compiler supports C99.*

3. *The arcsine and arccosine functions,* asin *and* acos, *are, respectively, the inverses of the* sin *and* cos *functions on a restricted domain. By experimenting, determine these restricted domains, i.e., the ranges of the* asin *and* acos *functions.*

4. *What values should* $\mathrm{asin}(x)$ *and* $\mathrm{acos}(x)$ *return if* x *is outside the range of the* sin *and* cos *functions? Check to see if your C math library does what you expected. The results may depend on whether your compiler supports C99.*

Exercise 10.12 *What is* $\mathrm{pow}(x,0)$ *when* x *is nonzero? What is* $\mathrm{pow}(0,x)$ *when* x *is nonzero? What is* $\mathrm{pow}(0,0)$? *What is the mathematical justification for these conventions? (See [Gol91].)*

Exercise 10.13 *It's unlikely that HAL, quoted on p. xiii, was IEEE compliant, since the movie* 2001: A Space Odyssey *predated the development of the standard by nearly two decades [Cla99]. What precision does HAL appear to be using? Does he report correctly rounded results for the square root and log functions before Dave starts dismantling his circuits? In order to answer this with certainty, you may need to use the* long double *versions of the math library functions, namely,* sqrtl, expl, *and* log10l. *If your system does not support these, you may want to use some other extended precision tool (see the end of Chapter* 13*).*

Exercise 10.14 *Recalling Exercise 6.12, is it possible that*

$$\text{sqrt}(x) \otimes \text{sqrt}(x) \tag{10.2}$$

or

$$\text{sqrt}(x \otimes x) \tag{10.3}$$

or

$$\exp(\log(x)) \tag{10.4}$$

or

$$\log(\exp(x)) \tag{10.5}$$

will not give the result x*, assuming that* x *is a positive floating point number and that neither overflow nor underflow takes place? Explain. Hint: One answer is quite different from the rest.*

Exercise 10.15 *For three out of the four expressions* (10.2), (10.3), (10.4), (10.5), *write a C program to find the smallest positive integer* x *for which the expression does not give the result* x*. Use double precision. If your program generates an apparently infinite loop, you picked the wrong expression. Explain your results.*

Exercise 10.16 *Repeat the previous experiment using single precision. You should assign intermediate results to* float *variables; for example, when computing* (10.2), *you should store the result* sqrt(x) *in a* float *variable before multiplying it by itself. Why is this? Explain your results.*

Exercise 10.17 *As mentioned in Chapter* 6, *interval arithmetic means floating point computing where, for each variable, lower and upper bounds on the exact value of the variable are maintained. This can be implemented using the* round down *and* round up *modes, assuming these are supported by your C compiler. Write a program to read a sequence of positive numbers and add them together in a sum. Include an option to set the rounding mode to any of* round down, round up, *and* round to nearest. *(If your compiler does not allow dynamic access to the rounding mode but does allow you to set the rounding mode before compilation, then make three different compiled versions of the program.) The* round down *mode should give you a lower bound on the exact result, the* round up *mode should give you an upper bound, and* round to nearest *should give you an intermediate result. Use type* float *but print the results to double precision so you can see the rounding effects clearly. Avoid using very simple input values (such as integers) that may not need rounding at all. Describe the results that you obtain. To how many digits do the three answers agree? The answer will depend on your data.*

Exercise 10.18 *If the rounding modes are supported by your C compiler, use the ideas of interval arithmetic (see previous exercise) to compute upper and lower bounds on the quantity*

$$\frac{a+b}{c+d},$$

where a, b, c, d are input values. Use float variables but print the results to double precision so you can see the effect of rounding. Think about how to do this carefully. Do you have to change the rounding mode dynamically, i.e., during the computation? (If so, but your compiler does not allow this, then find a way to work around the restriction, e.g., by writing temporary values to a file and breaking the program into several parts.) Be sure to try a variety of input data to fully test the program. Avoid using very simple input values (such as integers) that may not need rounding at all.

Exercise 10.19 Write a C program to compute (7.3), recovering from overflow or underflow as outlined at the end of Chapter 7. If your compiler supports C99, use the C99 macros [ISO99] to set and access the exception status flags. If your compiler does not support C99, you may still be able to write a working program by checking whether the computed results are either ∞ or 0 and, if they are, scaling and trying again. If your compiler does not support the macro INFINITY, then compute ∞ from $1.0/0.0$ at the beginning, assuming the standard response to division by zero is in effect. It may be helpful to look at a Fortran 2003 implementation [MRC04, Section 11.10.4].

Exercise 10.20 *Avoiding overflow in a product (J. Demmel).*

1. Write a C program to read a sequence of positive numbers and compute the product. Assume that the input numbers do not overflow the IEEE single format. The program should have the following properties:

   - The variables in the program should have type either float or int. Double or extended precision variables are not permitted.
   - The program should print the product of the numbers in the following nonstandard format: a floating point number F (in standard decimal exponential format), followed by the string

     `times 10 to the power`,

     followed by an integer K.
   - The result should not overflow, i.e., the result should not be ∞, even if the final value, or an intermediate value generated along the way, is bigger than $N_{\max}$, the biggest IEEE single format floating point number.
   - The program should be reasonably efficient, doing no unnecessary computation (except for comparisons) when none of the intermediate or final values are greater than $N_{\max}$. In this case, the integer K displayed should be zero.

   The way to accomplish these goals is as follows. Suppose the input consists of two numbers, both `1.0e30`, so that the product is too big to fit in the IEEE single floating point format. If the IEEE standard response to overflow is in effect, the result is ∞, and by observing this result the program can divide one of the numbers by a power of 10 and try again. By choosing the power of 10 correctly (possibly using a loop), the product can be made small enough not to overflow the IEEE single format. In this way, a final product is computed that requires final scaling by a certain power of 10: this is the integer that should be output, and you can assume this is not bigger than the biggest integer that can be stored. If your compiler does not support the macro INFINITY, then compute ∞ from $1.0/0.0$ at the beginning, assuming the standard response to division by zero is in effect.

   An important part of the assignment is to choose a good test set to properly check the program.

Note: When you multiply two numbers together and compare the result to ∞, you might not get the answer you expect unless you first store the product of the numbers in a float *variable (since the registers may use the double or extended format).*

2. *Extend the program so that the result does not underflow to zero regardless of how small the intermediate and final values are.*

3. *Should you also avoid underflow to subnormal intermediate and final values? Why or why not? How can this be done?*

4. *Make your program more efficient and accurate than outlined above. For example, scale by a power of 2 instead of 10. Then scaling introduces no rounding errors beyond the ones you can't avoid anyway. Decimal output can still be displayed at the end. Also, it is not efficient to scale by one power of 2 at a time; what would be a better choice? Instead of divisions, use multiplications by precomputed reciprocals, which is faster.*

Chapter 11

Cancellation

Consider the two numbers
$$x = 3.141592653589793$$
and
$$y = 3.141592653585682.$$
The first number, x, is a 16-digit approximation to π, while the second number agrees with π to only 12 digits. Their difference is
$$z = x - y = 0.000000000004111 = 4.111 \times 10^{-12}. \quad (11.1)$$

This difference is in the normalized range of the IEEE single format. However, if we compute the difference $z = x - y$ in a C program, using the single format to store the variables x and y before doing the subtraction, and display the result to single precision, we find that the result displayed for z is
$$\text{0.000000e+00}. \quad (11.2)$$

The reason is simple enough. The input numbers x and y are first converted from decimal to the single binary format; they are not exact floating point numbers, so the decimal to binary conversion requires some rounding. Because they agree to 12 digits, both x and y round to exactly the same single format number. Thus, all bits in their binary representation cancel when the subtraction is done; we say that we have a complete loss of accuracy in the computation $z = x - y$.

If we use the double format to store x and y and their difference z, and if we display the result to double precision, we find that z has the value
$$\text{4.110933815582030e-12}. \quad (11.3)$$

This agrees with the exact answer (11.1) to about four digits, but what is the meaning of the other digits? The answer is that the result displayed is the correctly rounded difference of the double format representations of x and y. Although we might prefer to see (11.1), this will not happen on a binary machine, as it would on a decimal calculator with enough digits. It is important to realize that in this case, we may ignore all but the first four or five digits of (11.3). The rest may be viewed as garbage, in the sense that they do not reflect the original data x and y. We say that we have a partial loss of accuracy in the computation $z = x - y$.

Regardless of whether the loss of accuracy is complete or partial, the phenomenon is called *cancellation*. It occurs when one number is subtracted from another number that is nearly equal to it. Equivalently, it occurs if two numbers with opposite sign but nearly equal magnitude are added together.

Approximating a Derivative by a Difference Quotient

An excellent illustration of cancellation is provided by the example of computing an approximation to a derivative. Let f be a continuously differentiable function of a single real variable, i.e., one for which the derivative f' exists and is continuous. Suppose that we do not have a formula for f, but only a program that evaluates $f(x)$ for any given value x. How would we estimate the value of $f'(x)$, the derivative of f at x?

By definition, $f'(x)$ is the slope of the line tangent to the graph of f at $(x, f(x))$, i.e., the limit of the difference quotient

$$\frac{f(x+h) - f(x)}{h} \qquad (11.4)$$

as h converges to zero. This difference quotient is the slope of the line passing through the points $(x+h, f(x+h))$ and $(x, f(x))$. A natural idea, then, is to evaluate (11.4) for some "small" value of h—but how small? Setting h to zero will give us $0/0$, i.e., NaN. Program 5 tries values of h ranging from 10^{-1} down to 10^{-20}, assuming that $x = 1$ and f is the sine function. Since we know that the derivative of $\sin(x)$ is $\cos(x)$, we can evaluate this at $x = 1$ and compare the result to the difference quotient. The absolute value of the difference between the two is called the *error*. The program uses type *double*.

```
#include <math.h>
main()   /* Program 5: Approximate a Derivative by a
                       Difference Quotient*/
{
   int n = 1;
   double x = 1.0, h = 1.0, deriv = cos(x), diffquo, error;

   printf(" deriv =%13.6e \n", deriv);
   printf("    h      diffquo    abs(deriv - diffquo) \n");

   /* Let h range from 10^{-1} down to 10^{-20} */

   while(n <= 20) {
      h = h/10;                              /* h = 10^(-n) */
      diffquo = (sin(x+h)-sin(x))/h;   /* difference quotient */
      error = fabs(deriv - diffquo);
      printf("%5.1e %13.6e %13.6e \n", h, diffquo, error);
      n++;
   }
}
```

Here is the output:

```
 deriv = 5.403023e-01
    h       diffquo     abs(deriv - diffquo)
1.0e-01   4.973638e-01    4.293855e-02
1.0e-02   5.360860e-01    4.216325e-03
1.0e-03   5.398815e-01    4.208255e-04
1.0e-04   5.402602e-01    4.207445e-05
1.0e-05   5.402981e-01    4.207362e-06
1.0e-06   5.403019e-01    4.207468e-07
```

CHAPTER 11. CANCELLATION

```
1.0e-07   5.403023e-01   4.182769e-08
1.0e-08   5.403023e-01   2.969885e-09
1.0e-09   5.403024e-01   5.254127e-08
1.0e-10   5.403022e-01   5.848104e-08
1.0e-11   5.403011e-01   1.168704e-06
1.0e-12   5.403455e-01   4.324022e-05
1.0e-13   5.395684e-01   7.339159e-04
1.0e-14   5.440093e-01   3.706976e-03
1.0e-15   5.551115e-01   1.480921e-02
1.0e-16   0.000000e+00   5.403023e-01
1.0e-17   0.000000e+00   5.403023e-01
1.0e-18   0.000000e+00   5.403023e-01
1.0e-19   0.000000e+00   5.403023e-01
1.0e-20   0.000000e+00   5.403023e-01
```

The error (the absolute value of `deriv - diffquo`) is plotted as a function of h in Figure 11.1, using a log–log scale. The results are quite interesting. We see that the approximation gets better, i.e., the error gets smaller, as h gets smaller—as we might expect—but only up to a certain point. When h gets *too* small, the approximation starts to get *worse!* Why?

After a little thought, the reason is clear. If $x = 1$ and h is smaller than half of

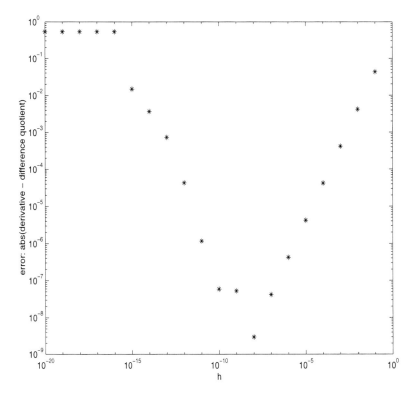

Figure 11.1: Error (Absolute Value of Derivative Minus Difference Quotient) as a Function of h (Log–Log Scale)

machine epsilon (about 10^{-16} in the double format), then $x+h$, i.e., $1+h$, is rounded to 1, and so naturally the formula that is being displayed gives the result zero, since the values $\sin(x+h)$ and $\sin(x)$ completely cancel. In other words, the final answer has *no significant digits*. When h is a *little* bigger than machine epsilon, the values do not completely cancel but they still *partially cancel*. For example, suppose that the first 10 digits of $\sin(x+h)$ and $\sin(x)$ are the same. Then, even though $\sin(x+h)$ and $\sin(x)$ both have about 16 significant digits, the difference has only about 6 significant digits. Since the difference is stored as a normalized double format number, it appears at first to have 16 significant digits, but only the first 6 are meaningful. We may summarize the situation by saying that using h too big gives a big *discretization error*, while using h too small gives a big *cancellation error*. For the function $f(x) = \sin(x)$ at $x = 1$, the best choice of h is about 10^{-8}, approximately *the square root of machine epsilon*.

A closer look at the output shows that, for the larger values of h, the error drops by approximately a factor of 10 every time h is reduced by a factor of 10—until the cancellation error starts to take over. There is a reason for this. To explain it, we assume that f is twice continuously differentiable, i.e., that the second derivative, f'', exists and is continuous—as is the case for the sine function. Then there exists z between x and $x+h$ such that

$$f(x+h) = f(x) + hf'(x) + \frac{h^2}{2}f''(z), \qquad (11.5)$$

where $f''(z)$ is the second derivative of f at z. Formula (11.5) is called a truncated Taylor series. Therefore,

$$\frac{f(x+h) - f(x)}{h} - f'(x) = \frac{h}{2}f''(z). \qquad (11.6)$$

This quantity is the difference between what we are computing, the difference quotient, and what we want, the exact derivative. Its absolute value is the *discretization error*. Equation (11.6) shows that if h is reduced by a factor of 10, the discretization error also decreases by a factor of about 10 (not exactly, since the point z between x and $x+h$ changes when h changes). Thus, we say the discretization error is $O(h)$. This explains the factors of 10 observed in the table (and the corresponding straight line of data on the right side of Figure 11.1).

The lesson to be learned here is that *cancellation*, which occurs when subtraction of nearly equal values takes place, should be avoided when possible. Using the formula for the derivative of a function is much more accurate than approximating it by difference quotients.

The Central Difference Quotient

As long as f is smooth enough, we can construct a more accurate approximation to the derivative of f at x by computing the slope of the line passing through $(x+h, f(x+h))$ and $(x-h, f(x-h))$, i.e.,

$$\frac{f(x+h) - f(x-h)}{2h}.$$

This is called the *central difference quotient*. Assume that the third derivative f''' exists and is continuous. For small enough h (but large enough that cancellation is not a problem), the central difference quotient gives a more accurate approximation to the derivative $f'(x)$ than the difference quotient (11.4). Here is the explanation. Truncated Taylor series give us

$$f(x+h) = f(x) + hf'(x) + \frac{h^2}{2}f''(x) + \frac{h^3}{6}f'''(z_1) \qquad (11.7)$$

CHAPTER 11. CANCELLATION

for some z_1 between x and $x + h$ and

$$f(x - h) = f(x) - hf'(x) + \frac{h^2}{2}f''(x) - \frac{h^3}{6}f'''(z_2) \tag{11.8}$$

for some z_2 between x and $x - h$. Subtracting (11.8) from (11.7) and dividing through by $2h$, we get

$$\frac{f(x + h) - f(x - h)}{2h} - f'(x) = \frac{h^2}{12}(f'''(z_1) + f'''(z_2)).$$

This gives the discretization error for the central difference quotient. Thus, the discretization error for the central difference quotient is $O(h^2)$ instead of $O(h)$.

Exercise 11.1 *Change Program 5 to use centered differences, and observe that when h is reduced by a factor of 10, the discretization error is reduced by a factor of about 100, confirming the $O(h^2)$ behavior. But, as before, when h becomes too small, the cancellation error dominates and the results become useless. Approximately what h gives the best results?*

Exercise 11.2 *Using a spreadsheet program such as Excel, implement the finite difference formula in a spreadsheet. Can you tell from the results what precision the spreadsheet program is using? If necessary, use the menu options to change the output format used.*

Chapter 12

Conditioning of Problems

Suppose we wish to solve some problem using numerical computing. Roughly speaking, the conditioning of the problem measures how accurately one can expect to be able to solve it using a given floating point precision, independently of the algorithm used. We confine our discussion to the problem of evaluating a real function of a real variable,

$$y = f(x),$$

assuming that f is twice continuously differentiable and that x and $f(x)$ are in the normalized range of the floating point precision. Define

$$\hat{x} = \text{round}(x).$$

Evaluating the function f on the computer using floating point arithmetic, the *best* we can hope for is to compute the value

$$\hat{y} = f(\hat{x}).$$

In fact, even this is an unreasonable hope because we will not be able to evaluate f exactly, but for simplicity, let us suppose for now that we can. Now, we know from (5.10) in Chapter 5 that the relative rounding error satisfies the bound

$$\frac{|\hat{x} - x|}{|x|} < \epsilon,$$

where ϵ is machine epsilon (with an additional factor of $1/2$ if the rounding mode is *round to nearest*). It follows that

$$-\log_{10}\left(\frac{|\hat{x} - x|}{|x|}\right) > -\log_{10}(\epsilon). \tag{12.1}$$

As noted in Chapter 5, the left-hand side of this inequality estimates the number of decimal digits to which $\hat{x}$ agrees with x—at least about seven digits in the case of IEEE single precision. The question we now ask is: To how many digits can we expect $\hat{y}$ to agree with y? To find out, we must look at the quantity

$$-\log_{10}\left(\frac{|\hat{y} - y|}{|y|}\right).$$

We have

$$\frac{\hat{y} - y}{y} = \frac{f(\hat{x}) - f(x)}{\hat{x} - x} \times \frac{x}{f(x)} \times \frac{\hat{x} - x}{x}. \tag{12.2}$$

The first factor,

$$\frac{f(\hat{x}) - f(x)}{\hat{x} - x}, \tag{12.3}$$

approximates $f'(x)$, the derivative of f at x. Therefore,

$$\frac{|\hat{y}-y|}{|y|} \approx \kappa_f(x) \times \frac{|\hat{x}-x|}{|x|}, \tag{12.4}$$

where

$$\kappa_f(x) = \frac{|x| \times |f'(x)|}{|f(x)|}. \tag{12.5}$$

The quantity $\kappa_f(x)$ is called the *condition number of f at x*. It measures *approximately* how much the relative rounding error in x is magnified by evaluation of f at x. (For a more rigorous derivation that eliminates the approximation symbol $\approx$, see Exercise 12.8.)

Now we are in a position to answer the question: To how many digits can we expect $\hat{y}$ to agree with y? The left-hand side of (12.4) is a relative measure of how well $\hat{y}$ approximates y. The second factor on the right-hand side of (12.4) is a relative measure of how well $\hat{x}$ approximates x. Taking logarithms (base 10) on both sides, we get

$$-\log_{10}\left(\frac{|\hat{y}-y|}{|y|}\right) \approx -\log_{10}\left(\frac{|\hat{x}-x|}{|x|}\right) - \log_{10}\left(\kappa_f(x)\right). \tag{12.6}$$

Here the left-hand side is approximately the number of digits to which $\hat{y}$ agrees with y, and the first term on the right-hand side is approximately the number of digits to which $\hat{x}$ agrees with x, which we know from (12.1) and Table 4.4 is at least about seven when IEEE single precision is in use. Consequently, we conclude with a rule of thumb.[21]

Rule of Thumb 12.1 *To estimate the number of digits to which $\hat{y} = f(\hat{x})$ agrees with $y = f(x)$, subtract*

$$\log_{10}\left(\kappa_f(x)\right)$$

from the approximate number of digits to which $\hat{x} = \text{round}(x)$ agrees with x, i.e., 7 when using IEEE single precision or 16 when using IEEE double precision (see Table 4.4). Here $\kappa_f(x)$ is the condition number of f at x, defined in (12.5), and we assume that f is twice continuously differentiable and that x and $f(x)$ are in the normalized range of the floating point system.

Since evaluating the condition number of f at x requires first evaluating f at x as well as the derivative $f'(x)$, the condition number does *not* help us solve our original problem, the evaluation of f. On the contrary, evaluating the condition number is harder than evaluating the function. However, the condition number *does* give us insight into difficulties that may arise when we evaluate f at certain values of x.

Exercise 12.1 *Determine the condition numbers of the functions*

$$g(x) = \frac{x}{10}$$

and

$$h(x) = x - 10,$$

and discuss what values of x, if any, give large condition numbers $\kappa_g(x)$ or $\kappa_h(x)$.

Table 12.1 tabulates the function, derivative, and condition number of three functions, the exponential, logarithmic, and sine functions, each at three different values of x. These values are all exact. The three functions and the relevant points $(x, f(x))$ are shown in Figure 12.1. The derivatives of $\exp(x)$, $\log(x)$, and $\sin(x)$ are

$$\exp(x), \quad \frac{1}{x}, \quad \cos(x),$$

---
[21] A rule of thumb is any method of measuring that is practical though not precise [Web96].

CHAPTER 12. CONDITIONING OF PROBLEMS

Table 12.1: Sample Condition Numbers

f	x	$f(x)$	$f'(x)$	$\kappa_f(x)$	$\log_{10}(\kappa_f(x))$
exp	1	e	e	1	0
exp	0	1	1	0	$-\infty$
exp	-1	$1/e$	$1/e$	1	0
log	e	1	$1/e$	1	0
log	1	0	1	∞	∞
log	$1/e$	-1	e	1	0
sin	π	0	-1	∞	∞
sin	$\pi/2$	1	0	0	$-\infty$
sin	0	0	1	NaN	NaN

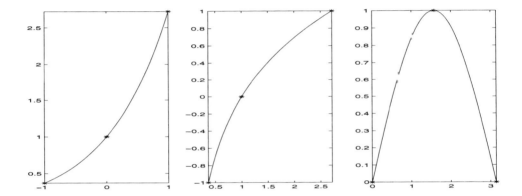

Figure 12.1: Exponential, Logarithmic, and Sine Functions

respectively, so the condition numbers are

$$\kappa_{\exp}(x) = |x|, \quad \kappa_{\log}(x) = \frac{1}{|\log(x)|}, \quad \kappa_{\sin}(x) = \frac{|x|}{|\tan(x)|}. \tag{12.7}$$

Altogether, Table 12.1 gives nine examples. Four of these examples have condition numbers equal to 1. In these examples, we expect that if $\hat{x}$ approximates x to about seven significant digits, then $\hat{y} = f(\hat{x})$ should approximate $y = f(x)$ to about seven digits. In two examples, we see a condition number equal to 0. The problem of evaluating $f(x)$ in these examples is said to be *infinitely well conditioned*, and we expect that $\hat{y}$ should approximate y to *many more* digits than $\hat{x}$ approximates x. On the other hand, two other examples have condition numbers equal to ∞. The problem of evaluating $f(x)$ in these cases is said to be *infinitely ill conditioned*, and we expect that $\hat{y}$ should approximate y to *many fewer* digits than $\hat{x}$ approximates x. Finally, there is one case in which the condition number is not defined because both x and $f(x)$ are zero. This is indicated by the NaN in the table. However, see Exercise 12.3.

Exercise 12.2 *Construct a table like Table 12.1 to display the condition number of the functions* log10, cos, *and* asin, *using points where they can be computed exactly, if possible.*

Exercise 12.3 *The condition number of the sine function is not defined at $x = 0$, but the limit of the condition number is defined as $x \to 0$. What is this limit? Does (12.4) still hold if we define this limit to be the condition number?*

Checking the Rule of Thumb

We used Program 6 to evaluate the math library functions exp, log, and sin near the points x shown in Table 12.1. The values e, $1/e$, π, and $\pi/2$ were input to *double* accuracy and stored in the *double* variable xD. The values 1, 0, and -1 would have been stored exactly, so instead we input numbers *near* these values. For each input value, Program 6 computes the relevant function value in two ways. The output is summarized in Table 12.2. The fourth column displays the *double* results computed by the function when its argument is the *double* variable xD. The third column displays the *double* results computed by the function when its argument is *rounded to single precision before being passed to the function*. In both cases, the function evaluation uses double precision and the value is displayed to 16 digits. The only difference is the precision of the *argument passed to the function*.

```
#include <math.h>
main ()      /* Program 6: Function Evaluation */
{
   int funcode;                         /* function code */
   float xS;                            /* IEEE single */
   double xD, fxS, fxD, relerr, cond;   /* IEEE double */

   printf("enter 1 for exp, 2 for log, 3 for sin ");
   scanf("%d", &funcode);
   printf("enter an input value \n");
   scanf("%lf", &xD);      /* read using double format */
   xS = xD;                /* force single format */
   switch (funcode) {
      case 1: fxS = exp(xS); fxD = exp(xD);
                             cond = fabs(xD); break;
      case 2: fxS = log(xS); fxD = log(xD);
                             cond = fabs(1/log(xD)); break;
      case 3: fxS = sin(xS); fxD = sin(xD);
                             cond = fabs(xD/tan(xD)); break;
   }
   printf("funcode %d\n", funcode);
   printf("xS = %22.15e   f(xS) = %22.15e \n", xS, fxS);
   printf("xD = %22.15e   f(xD) = %22.15e \n", xD, fxD);
   /* relative error */
   relerr = fabs((fxD - fxS)/fxD);
   /* approximate number of digits they are in agreement */
   printf("relative error    = %e   ", relerr);
   printf("approx digits agreeing = %2.0f\n", -log10(relerr));
   /* log base 10 of condition number */
   printf("condition number = %e   ", cond);
   printf("log10 condition number = %2.0f\n", log10(cond));
}
```

We may view the numbers in the third column of Table 12.2 as reasonably accurate evaluations of $\hat{y}$, the value of the function f at its rounded-to-single argument $\hat{x}$. We

Table 12.2: Actual Function Evaluations: Exp, Log, and Sin

f	x	$f(x)$, x rounded to single	$f(x)$, x rounded to double	Agree	Loss
exp	1.000001	2.718284420815846e+00	2.718284546742233e+00	7	0
exp	0.000001	1.000001000000498e+00	1.000001000000500e+00	15	−6
exp	−1.000001	3.678790903344350e−01	3.678790732921851e−01	7	0
log	e (double)	9.999999696321400e−01	1.000000000000000e+00	8	0
log	1.001	9.995470164405893e−04	9.995003330834232e−04	4	3
log	1.000001	9.536738616591883e−07	9.999994999180668e−07	1	6
log	$1/e$ (double)	−9.999999751283870e−01	−1.000000000000000e+00	8	0
sin	π (double)	−8.742278000372475e−08	1.224646799147353e−16	−9	16
sin	$\pi/2$ (double)	9.999999999999990e−01	1.000000000000000e+00	15	−15
sin	0.000001	9.999999974750761e−07	9.999999999998333e−07	9	0

may view the numbers in the fourth column as reasonably accurate evaluations of the exact value $y = f(x)$—at least, the rounded-to-double argument xD is much closer to the input value x than the rounded-to-single argument xS. The column headed Agree in Table 12.1 estimates the number of digits to which these two computations agree, using the formula on the left-hand side of (12.6), rounded to the nearest integer. The column headed Loss shows the log (base 10) of the condition number of the function at xD, using (12.7) and rounding to the nearest integer. According to Rule of Thumb 12.1, the number shown in the column headed Agree should be approximately 7 minus the number shown in the column headed Loss. This is exactly the case for several of the input values, e.g., the log function at $x = 1.001$ (where the condition number is about 1000) and $x = 1.000001$ (where it is about 10^6). These are two of the ill-conditioned examples. In the extremely well-conditioned cases, the exp function at $x = 10^{-6}$ (condition number 10^{-6}) and the sine function very near $\pi/2$ (condition number 10^{-15}), we have, as expected, more agreement in the function values than there is in their arguments; however, this is limited to about 15 digits, about the most we can expect using double precision computations. In the case of the sine function near π, which is the worst conditioned example of all (condition number 10^{16}), the displayed agreement of -9 digits is a consequence of the division by fxD in the computation of the log (base 10) of the relative error; if we divided by fxS instead, we would be informed that we have 0 digits of agreement.

Exercise 12.4 *As mentioned in Chapter 4, deciding to how many digits two numbers agree is problematic. Devise a rule that you think is reasonable and test it on the numbers in Table 12.2. How do your answers compare with the log (base 10) of the relative error reported in the column headed Agree?*

Exercise 12.5 *Modify Program 6 to evaluate the functions whose condition numbers were displayed in Exercise 12.2, and display the results in a table like Table 12.2. Don't forget to use the correct formulas for the condition numbers defining the output for the Loss column. Do the results support Rule of Thumb 12.1?*

Exercise 12.6 *Determine the condition number of the parallel resistance formula with variable R_1 and fixed $R_2 = 1$, i.e., the condition number of*

$$f(x) = \frac{1}{\frac{1}{x} + 1}.$$

Exercise 12.7 *Suppose that g is a function that is three times continuously differentiable. Determine the condition number for the problem of evaluating the exact derivative*
$$f(x) = g'(x)$$
and the condition number for evaluating the exact difference quotient
$$f_h(x) = \frac{g(x+h) - g(x)}{h}$$
for fixed $h > 0$. Does the latter converge to the former as h converges to zero?

Exercise 12.8 *Replace (12.4) by a more precise statement that does not use the $\approx$ symbol, using the truncated Taylor series (11.5) instead of (11.4) together with the assumption that f is twice continuously differentiable.*

The notion of conditioning extends far beyond simple function evaluation to more complicated and challenging problems. In other settings, the definition of condition number is more subtle than (12.5). For example, suppose the problem to be solved is to compute $y = Ax$, where A is a matrix and x is a vector, or to solve a system of linear equations $Ay = x$ for y, where A is a square nonsingular matrix and x is a vector. If we take A to be fixed, we need to know how relative errors in the solution vector y depend on relative errors in the data vector x, where we must introduce the notion of a *norm* to quantify the magnitude of a vector. The condition number is then defined to measure the *worst case* of such dependence over all data vectors x with fixed norm; see [Dem97], [Hig96], or [TB97]. In the case of simple function evaluation discussed in this chapter, where x is a scalar, not a vector, this crucial worst case aspect of the condition number is not present.

Chapter 13

Stability of Algorithms

An algorithm is a well-defined computational method to solve a given class of problems. In computer science, the study of algorithms is traditionally concerned with efficiency; it is understood that an algorithm is supposed to get the correct answer, though proving that this will happen is not necessarily easy. However, numerical algorithms, which solve problems using floating point arithmetic, almost never find the exact solution to a problem. Instead, the goal is "approximately correct" answers. These are by no means guaranteed. Although each individual floating point operation is correctly rounded, a poor choice of algorithm may introduce unnecessarily large rounding errors.

We saw in the previous chapter that the conditioning of a problem measures how accurately one can expect to be able to solve it using a given floating point precision, independently of the algorithm used. The stability of an algorithm measures how good a job the algorithm does at solving problems to the achievable accuracy defined by their conditioning. For whatever problem one might want to solve, some algorithms are better than others. Those algorithms that get *unnecessarily inaccurate* answers are called *unstable*.

We continue to confine our attention to the problem of evaluating a real function of a real variable,

$$y = f(x),$$

assuming that f is twice continuously differentiable and that x and $f(x)$ are in the normalized range of the floating point precision. As earlier, define

$$\hat{x} = \text{round}(x).$$

We commented in the previous chapter that, using floating point arithmetic, the *best* we can hope for is to compute the value

$$\hat{y} = f(\hat{x}), \tag{13.1}$$

and we showed that

$$\frac{|\hat{y} - y|}{|y|} \approx \kappa_f(x) \frac{|\hat{x} - x|}{|x|},$$

where $\kappa_f(x)$ is the condition number of f at x. However, it is generally too much to expect an algorithm to find $\hat{y}$ satisfying (13.1). We say that an algorithm to compute $f(x)$ is *stable* if it returns $\tilde{y}$ satisfying

$$\frac{|\tilde{y} - y|}{|y|} \approx \kappa_f(x) \frac{|\hat{x} - x|}{|x|}, \tag{13.2}$$

where, as earlier, we deliberately avoid a specific definition for the symbol ≈, meaning approximately equal. For rigorous definitions of stability, see [TB97, Section III] and [Hig96, Chapter 1]. Note that we do not insist that $\tilde{y} = f(\hat{x})$.[22] If an algorithm to compute $f(x)$ delivers $\tilde{y}$ for which the left-hand side of (13.2) is much greater than the right-hand side, we say the algorithm is *unstable*.

Compound Interest

We illustrate these concepts by considering algorithms for computing compound interest. Suppose we invest a_0 dollars in a bank that pays 5% interest per year, compounded quarterly. This means that at the end of the first quarter of the year, the value of our investment is
$$a_1 = a_0 \times (1 + (.05)/4)$$
dollars, i.e., the original amount plus one quarter of 5% of the original amount. At the end of the second quarter, the bank pays interest not only on the original amount a_0, but also on the interest earned in the first quarter; thus, the value of the investment at the end of the second quarter is
$$a_2 = a_1 \times (1 + (.05)/4) = a_0 \times (1 + (.05)/4)^2$$
dollars. At the end of the third quarter the bank pays interest on this amount, so that the investment is now worth
$$a_3 = a_2 \times (1 + (.05)/4) = a_0 \times (1 + (.05)/4)^3,$$
and at the end of the whole year the bank pays the last installment of interest on the amount a_3, so that the investment is finally worth
$$a_4 = a_3 \times (1 + (.05)/4) = a_0 \times (1 + (.05)/4)^4.$$
In general, if a_0 dollars are invested at an interest rate x with compounding n times per year, at the end of the year the final value is
$$a_0 \times C_n(x)$$
dollars, where
$$C_n(x) = \left(1 + \frac{x}{n}\right)^n.$$
This is the *compound interest formula*. It is well known that, for fixed x, the compound interest formula $C_n(x)$ has a limiting value as $n \to \infty$, namely, $\exp(x)$, as already displayed in (10.1). Consequently, excessively high compounding frequencies are pointless.

Nonetheless, it is interesting to evaluate $C_n(x)$ for various choices of n. Before considering algorithms to do this, let us investigate the condition number of $C_n(x)$. From the chain rule, the derivative is
$$C_n'(x) = n \left(1 + \frac{x}{n}\right)^{n-1} \cdot \frac{1}{n} = \frac{C_n(x)}{1 + \frac{x}{n}}.$$
Thus, for n sufficiently large compared to $|x|$, $C_n(x)$ is close to being its own derivative, which is not surprising, since the derivative of the limiting function $\exp(x)$ is itself. Therefore, the condition number of C_n is
$$\kappa_{C_n}(x) = \frac{|x|}{|C_n(x)|} \times \frac{|C_n(x)|}{|1 + \frac{x}{n}|} = \frac{|x|}{|1 + \frac{x}{n}|},$$
which converges to $|x|$, the condition number of $\exp(x)$ (see (12.7)), as $n \to \infty$.

---

[22]The more demanding definition known as *backward stability* requires that $\tilde{y} = f(\tilde{x})$ for some $\tilde{x}$ relatively close to x.

CHAPTER 13. STABILITY OF ALGORITHMS

Consequently, the compound interest formula is a well-conditioned function even for very large n, as long as $|x|$ is not large.

We first state the simplest, though not the most efficient, algorithm for computing $C_n(x)$.

Algorithm 13.1

1. Compute $z = 1 + \frac{x}{n}$, and set $w = 1$.
2. Repeatedly (n times) perform the multiplication $w \leftarrow w \times z$, and return w.

Since n may be large, the following more efficient algorithm makes use of the C library function **pow**.

Algorithm 13.2

1. Compute $z = 1 + \frac{x}{n}$.
2. Return $\text{pow}(z, n)$.

A third algorithm makes use of the properties of the exponential and logarithmic functions. Writing
$$C_n(x) = z^n$$
and taking logarithms (base e) of both sides, we obtain
$$\log C_n(x) = n \times \log(z).$$
Therefore,
$$C_n(x) = \exp(n \times \log(z)).$$

Algorithm 13.3

1. Compute $z = 1 + \frac{x}{n}$.
2. Compute $v = \log(z)$ and return $\exp(n \times v)$.

Program 7 implements all three algorithms in C using single precision. The output for various n is summarized in Table 13.1. In all cases the input for x is 0.05, i.e., an interest rate of 5%.

```
#include <math.h>
main ()     /* Program 7: Compound Interest */
{
    int n,i;
    float x,z,w,v;

    printf("enter input values for x (float) and n (integer) \n");
    scanf("%f  %d", &x, &n );
    z = 1 + x/n;
    w = 1;
    for (i=0; i<n; i++) {
        w = w*z;
    }
    v = log(z);
    printf("Alg 1: %e \n", w);
    printf("Alg 2: %e \n", pow(z,n));
    printf("Alg 3: %e \n", exp(n*v));
}
```

Table 13.1: Compound Interest at 5%, Single Precision

n	Algorithm 13.1	Algorithm 13.2	Algorithm 13.3
4	1.050946	1.050946	1.050946
365	1.051262	1.051262	1.051262
1000	1.051215	1.051216	1.051216
10,000	1.051331	1.051342	1.051342
100,000	1.047684	1.048839	1.048839
1,000,000	1.000000	1.000000	1.000000

The results are alarming! They look reasonable only for $n = 4$ (compounding quarterly) and $n = 365$ (compounding daily). For $n = 1000$, all three algorithms give results that are *less* than the result for $n = 365$. This is certainly not correct; we know that compounding more often may not give much more interest, but it certainly should not give less! We get our first clue as to what is happening when we come to the last line in the table. When $n = 1,000,000$, the computation in step 1 of all three algorithms,

$$z = 1 + \frac{.05}{1000000},$$

rounds exactly to 1 using single precision. Thus, the crucial interest rate information is completely lost, and all three algorithms return a result exactly equal to 1, as if the interest rate had been zero. Likewise, when $n = 10,000$ or $n = 100,000$, *some* but not *all* of the interest rate information is being lost in the computation of z.

On the other hand, it is clear that z is being computed correctly to about seven digits—there is no cancellation here! So why does the loss of the subsequent digits matter?

The heart of the matter is that *all three algorithms are unstable*. The rounding error in step 1 of each algorithm has a dramatically bad effect because the condition number of the function being computed in step 2 is *much worse* than the condition number of C_n. In fact, step 2 of all three algorithms computes the same function,

$$P_n(z) = z^n.$$

The derivative of $P_n(z)$ is nz^{n-1}, so the condition number is

$$\kappa_{P_n}(z) = \frac{|z \times nz^{n-1}|}{|z^n|} = n,$$

which, unlike the condition number of $C_n(x)$, grows without bound as $n \to \infty$. For example, when $n = 100,000$, the log (base 10) of the condition number is 5, and so, according to Rule of Thumb 12.1, although z computed in step 1 has seven significant digits, the result w computed in step 2 has only about two accurate digits. Thus, ill conditioning has been introduced, even though it was not present in the original function to be computed. Consequently, the algorithms are unstable.

Algorithm 13.3 does not avoid the instability with its use of exp and log. We already observed in the previous chapter that $\log(z)$ has a large condition number near $z = 1$, so although z is accurate to about seven digits, $v = \log(z)$ is accurate to only about two digits when $x = .05$ and $n = 100,000$ (see Table 12.2).

The easiest way to get more accurate answers is to change Program 7 so that all computations are done in double precision. All we need to do is change float

CHAPTER 13. STABILITY OF ALGORITHMS

Table 13.2: Compound Interest at 5%

n	Algorithm 13.1 (double)	Algorithm 13.2 (double)	Algorithm 13.3 (double)	Algorithm 13.4 (single)
4	1.050945	1.050945	1.050945	1.050945
365	1.051267	1.051267	1.051267	1.051267
1000	1.051270	1.051270	1.051270	1.051270
10,000	1.051271	1.051271	1.051271	1.051271
100,000	1.051271	1.051271	1.051271	1.051271
1,000,000	1.051271	1.051271	1.051271	1.051271

to double, and change %f to %lf in the scanf statement. The results, shown in Table 13.2, are correct to single precision accuracy because we are doing the computations in double precision. Of course, the algorithms are still not stable. If n is sufficiently large, inaccurate answers will again appear.

Exercise 13.1 *For what n does the double precision version of Program 7 give poor answers? Display the results in a table like Table 13.1.*

Surprisingly, there is no obvious stable algorithm to compute the compound interest formula using only the library functions pow, exp, and log. See [Gol91] for a simple stable algorithm that uses only exp and log, but one that is clever and far from obvious; a related discussion is given in [Hig96, Section 1.14.1]. However, C99 provides a math library function log1p that is exactly what we need:

$$\mathrm{log1p}(s) = \log(1+s).$$

This function is well-conditioned at and near $s = 0$ (see Exercise 13.2). This eliminates the need for the addition in step 1 of Algorithm 13.3 and gives us the following stable algorithm.

Algorithm 13.4

1. Compute $u = \frac{x}{n}$.

2. Compute $v = \mathrm{log1p}(u)$, and return $\exp(n \times v)$.

This is implemented in Program 8, and the results are shown in Table 13.2. The stable algorithm gives accurate results using single precision; the unstable algorithms give such accurate results only when double precision is used.

```
#include <math.h>
main ()      /* Program 8: Stable Algorithm for Compound Interest */
{
   int n;
   float x,u,v;

   printf("enter input values for x (float) and n (integer) \n");
   scanf("%f  %d", &x, &n );
   u = x/n;
   v = log1p(u);
   printf("Alg 4: %e \n", exp(n*v));
}
```

Exercise 13.2 *What is condition number of the function* $\text{log1p}(s)$ *as a function of* s? *What is the limit of the condition number as* $s \to 0$? *See Exercise 12.3.*

Instability via Cancellation

In fact, the phenomenon of cancellation described in Chapter 11 can be completely explained by conditioning. The condition number of the function

$$f(x) = x - 1$$

is

$$\kappa_f(x) = \frac{|x|}{|x - 1|},$$

which is arbitrarily large for x close to 1. Consequently, an algorithm that introduces cancellation unnecessarily is introducing ill conditioning unnecessarily and is unstable.

In Chapter 11, we discussed the idea of approximating a derivative $g'(x)$ by a difference quotient. A working of Exercise 12.7 shows that the problem of evaluating the difference quotient has the same condition number in the limit as $h \to 0$ as the problem of evaluating $g'(x)$ directly. Suppose that this condition number is not large. Unfortunately, the first step in evaluating the difference quotient, computing $g(x+h) - g(x)$, *does* have a large condition number for small h, and hence computing the difference quotient without the use of intermediate higher precision is unstable. Better algorithms exist to approximate the derivative, e.g., using the central difference quotient with larger h or still more accurate difference quotients with still larger h. However, this does not mean that the ordinary difference quotient is necessarily a poor choice of algorithm, as it may be justified by its efficiency and may be adequate if h is chosen carefully. Of course, using the formula for the derivative is preferable if it is known.

Exercise 13.3 *Why is the formula*

$$\frac{x^2 - 1}{x - 1}$$

an unstable way to compute $f(x) = x + 1$? *For what values of* x *is it unstable?*

Exercise 13.4 *Consider the function* $f(x) = \exp(x) - 1$.

1. *What is the condition number of* $f(x)$? *What is the limit of the condition number as* $x \to 0$? *See Exercise 12.3.*

2. *Write a C program to compute* $f(x)$ *using the exp function. Is the algorithm stable? If not, what are the values of* x *that cause trouble?*

3. *If your compiler supports C99, write a C program to compute* $f(x)$ *directly by calling the math library function* `expm1`, *intended exactly for this purpose. Does it give more accurate results?*

Exercise 13.5 *This is an extension to Exercise 10.17. Instead of using only positive input data, run your interval sum program to add up numbers with both positive and negative values. Choose some of your input values so that the numbers cancel out and the result is zero or close to zero. To how many significant digits do your three answers (upper bound, lower bound, and intermediate) agree? Is it as many as before? Is the difficulty that the problem of adding data with alternating signs is* ill conditioned, *or that the addition algorithm is* unstable? *Does it help to add up the positive and*

CHAPTER 13. STABILITY OF ALGORITHMS

negative terms separately? Be sure to try a variety of input data to fully test the program.

Computing the Exponential Function without a Math Library

For our second example illustrating stability and instability, let us attempt to compute the exponential function $\exp(x)$ directly, without any calls to library functions. From (12.7), we know that exp is a well-conditioned function as long as $|x|$ is not too large. We use the well-known Taylor series

$$\exp(x) = 1 + x + \frac{x^2}{2!} + \frac{x^3}{3!} + \cdots.$$

This allows us to approximately compute the limiting sum by means of a simple loop, noting that successive terms are related by

$$\frac{x^n}{n!} = \left(\frac{x^{n-1}}{(n-1)!}\right) \times \frac{x}{n}.$$

Thus, each term is easily computed from the previous term by multiplying by x and dividing by n. How should we terminate the loop? The simplest way would be to continue until the new term in the sum underflows to zero, as in Program 2 (Chapter 10). A better solution is to use the idea in Program 3 (Chapter 10): the loop may be terminated when *the new term is small enough that adding it to the previous terms does not change the sum*. Program 9 implements this idea using single precision.

```
#include <math.h>
main()   /* Program 9: Compute exp(x) from its Taylor series */
{
   int n;
   float x, term, oldsum, newsum;

   printf("Enter x \n");
   scanf("%e", &x);
   n = 0;
   oldsum = 0.0;
   newsum = 1.0;
   term = 1.0;
   /* terminates when the new sum is no different from the old sum */
   while (newsum !=oldsum){
      oldsum = newsum;
      n++;
      term = term*x/n;    /* term has the value (x^n)/(n!) */
      newsum = newsum + term;  /* approximates exp(x) */
      printf("n = %3d   term = %13.6e   newsum = %13.6e \n",
             n,term,newsum);
   }
   printf("From summing the series,    exp(x)=%e \n", newsum);
   printf("Using the standard function, exp(x)=%e \n", exp(x));
}
```

Here is the output of Program 9 for $x = .05$:

```
n =   1    term =   5.000000e-02    newsum =   1.050000e+00
n =   2    term =   1.250000e-03    newsum =   1.051250e+00
n =   3    term =   2.083333e-05    newsum =   1.051271e+00
n =   4    term =   2.604167e-07    newsum =   1.051271e+00
n =   5    term =   2.604167e-09    newsum =   1.051271e+00
From summing the series,     exp(x)=1.051271e+00
Using the standard function, exp(x)=1.051271e+00
```

We see that the value of **term** printed at each step grows rapidly smaller, and the loop terminates when **term** is so small that two successive values of **newsum** are identical. Actually, it looks from the output that this occurs a few lines before the loop terminates, but that is just the decimal conversion of **newsum** to seven digits; the binary floating point values are different until the last line. The final value of **newsum**, 1.051271, agrees with the value computed by the library function **exp** to all digits shown.

Now let us run Program 9 again for a larger value of x, say 10.0:

```
n =   1    term =   1.000000e+01    newsum =   1.100000e+01
n =   2    term =   5.000000e+01    newsum =   6.100000e+01
n =   3    term =   1.666667e+02    newsum =   2.276667e+02

..........4 lines omitted..........

n =   8    term =   2.480159e+03    newsum =   7.330842e+03
n =   9    term =   2.755732e+03    newsum =   1.008657e+04
n =  10    term =   2.755732e+03    newsum =   1.284231e+04
n =  11    term =   2.505211e+03    newsum =   1.534752e+04
n =  12    term =   2.087676e+03    newsum =   1.743519e+04
n =  13    term =   1.605905e+03    newsum =   1.904110e+04
n =  14    term =   1.147075e+03    newsum =   2.018817e+04
n =  15    term =   7.647164e+02    newsum =   2.095289e+04

..........13 lines omitted..........

n =  29    term =   1.130996e-02    newsum =   2.202646e+04
n =  30    term =   3.769987e-03    newsum =   2.202647e+04
n =  31    term =   1.216125e-03    newsum =   2.202647e+04
n =  32    term =   3.800390e-04    newsum =   2.202647e+04
From summing the series,     exp(x)=2.202647e+04
Using the standard function, exp(x)=2.202647e+04
```

We find that **term** grows larger than its initial value before it starts to get smaller, but it does eventually grow smaller when $n > 10$, and the loop eventually terminates as before, with an answer 22026.47 that again agrees with the library function **exp** to single precision.

Exercise 13.6 *Termination of the loop takes place when the decimal exponents of* **newsum** *and* **term** *differ by about 7 or 8. Why is this?*

Table 13.3 shows the output of Program 9 for various values of x. The first column shows the value computed by summing the series, and the second column shows the

CHAPTER 13. STABILITY OF ALGORITHMS

Table 13.3: Computing the Exponential Function

x	Computed by summing series	Computed by call to exp(x)
10	2.202647e+04	2.202647e+04
1	2.718282e+00	2.718282e+00
.05	1.051271e+00	1.051271e+00
-1	3.678794e-01	3.678794e-01
-5	6.738423e-03	6.737947e-03
-10	-6.256183e-05	4.539993e-05

result returned by the library function exp. The results agree to single precision for $x = 10$, $x = 1$, $x = 0.05$, and $x = -1$. However, the final line of Table 13.3 shows that the value computed by the loop for $x = -10$ is completely wrong! And the previous line for $x = -5$ is correct to only about four digits.

Let's look at the details for $x = -10$.

```
n =    1    term = -1.000000e+01    newsum = -9.000000e+00
n =    2    term =  5.000000e+01    newsum =  4.100000e+01

..........6 lines omitted..........

n =    9    term = -2.755732e+03    newsum = -1.413145e+03
n =   10    term =  2.755732e+03    newsum =  1.342587e+03

.........34 lines omitted..........

n =   45    term = -8.359650e-12    newsum = -6.256183e-05
n =   46    term =  1.817315e-12    newsum = -6.256183e-05
From summing the series,      exp(x)=-6.256183e-05
Using the standard function, exp(x)=4.539993e-05
```

We see that the values of term are the same as for $x = 10$ except that they alternate in sign, which makes sense, since when n is odd,

$$\frac{(-x)^n}{n!} = \frac{-(x^n)}{n!}.$$

Therefore, since the terms alternate in sign, they cancel with each other, and eventually the value of newsum starts to get smaller. The final result is a small number; this is to be expected, since $\exp(x) < 1$ for $x < 0$. Also, the loop takes longer to terminate than it did for $x = 10$, since the decimal exponents of term and newsum must differ by about 7 or 8 and newsum is smaller than it was before. Looking at the final value for newsum, however, we see that the answer is completely wrong, since it is not possible for $\exp(x)$ to be negative for any value of x. What is happening?

To find out, we examine the line-by-line output of Program 9 more carefully. We see that for $x = -10$, the size (i.e., absolute value) of term increases to 2.75×10^3 (for $n = 10$) before it starts decreasing to zero. We know that term is accurate to at most about seven digits, since it is an IEEE single format number. Consequently, its largest value, about 2.75×10^3, must have an absolute rounding error that is at least about 10^{-4}. The same error must be present in newsum, since it is obtained by adding values of term together. As more terms are added to newsum, this error is *not* reduced, even though the value of newsum continues to get smaller as the terms cancel each other out. In fact, the final value of newsum is smaller, in absolute value, than the error and consequently has *no significant digits*. The source of the difficulty is the size of the intermediate results together with the alternating sign of the terms, which cancel each other out, leading to a small final result even though the individual terms are quite large. For $x > 0$, there is no difficulty, since all the terms are positive and no cancellation takes place. But for $x < 0$, the results are meaningless for $|x|$ sufficiently large.

Now let's run Program 9 for $x = -5$:

```
n =   1    term =  -5.000000e+00    newsum =  -4.000000e+00
n =   2    term =   1.250000e+01    newsum =   8.500000e+00
n =   3    term =  -2.083333e+01    newsum =  -1.233333e+01
n =   4    term =   2.604167e+01    newsum =   1.370833e+01
n =   5    term =  -2.604167e+01    newsum =  -1.233333e+01
n =   6    term =   2.170139e+01    newsum =   9.368057e+00

        .........20 lines omitted..........

n =  27    term =  -6.842382e-10    newsum =   6.738423e-03
n =  28    term =   1.221854e-10    newsum =   6.738423e-03
From summing the series,    exp(x)=6.738423e-03
Using the standard function, exp(x)=6.737947e-03
```

The final result agrees with the library function exp to a few digits, but not to full precision. When $x = -5$, the difficulty is not as severe, since the size of term grows only to 2.6×10^1 before it starts decreasing to 0. This value of term, which is again accurate to at most about seven digits, has an absolute rounding error at least about 10^{-6}. The final answer, which is computed to be 6.738423×10^{-3}, must have an error of size at least about 10^{-6} and is therefore accurate to only about three digits.

Since the problem of computing $\exp(x)$ is well conditioned when $|x|$ is not large, the inevitable conclusion is that Program 9 implements an algorithm that is unstable for $x < 0$.

How can we change Program 9 so that it is stable? The answer is simple: if x is negative, sum the series for the positive value $-x$ and compute the reciprocal of the final amount, using the fact that

$$\exp(x) = \frac{1}{\exp(-x)}. \tag{13.3}$$

Thus we add to the end of the code

```
printf("One over the sum=%e \n", 1/newsum);
printf("Call to exp(-x) =%e \n", exp(-x));
```

and run it for $x = 10$ instead of $x = -10$. The final two lines of output are

```
One over the sum=4.539992e-05
Call to exp(-x) =4.539993e-05
```

It may seem amazing that this simple trick could work so well, but the reason it works is that *no cancellation takes place*. Dividing 1 by a large number with about six or seven significant digits results in a small number that also has about six or seven significant digits. (See Exercise 13.7.)

This confirms that the difficulty with Program 9 was not inherent in the problem that it solves, which is not ill conditioned. We chose an unstable algorithm that introduced cancellation, and therefore ill conditioning, unnecessarily.

Although Program 9 works well when cancellation is avoided, it cannot be concluded that summing a series until the sum is unchanged will always give such good answers. See Exercises 13.13–13.15.

The library function exp uses a more clever but more complicated method, which is both highly accurate and very fast. The purpose of this discussion has been to show that a good answer can be obtained with a simple program, but also that a completely wrong answer can be obtained if precautions are not taken. For much more detailed— yet very readable—discussions of algorithms for computing the functions in the math library, see [Mul97].

Some microprocessors provide hardware implementations of some of the math functions. For example, the Intel microprocessors provide hardware support for base 2 exponential and logarithmic functions.

Exercise 13.7 *Determine the condition number of the function*

$$f(x) = \frac{1}{x}.$$

Are there any finite, nonzero numbers x for which f has a large condition number?

Exercise 13.8 *Suppose Program 9 is changed to use double precision. For what range of values of x (approximately) does it give no significant digits, and why? Modify Program 9 further using the formula (13.3) to correct the difficulty.*

Exercise 13.9 *Suppose Program 9 is changed to add the positive and negative terms in two separate sums, and take their difference at the end. Does this improve its stability? Why or why not?*

Exercise 13.10 *If $|x|$ is large enough, overflow occurs in Program 9. If the standard response to overflow is used, what results are generated (a) if $x > 0$, (b) if $x < 0$, and (c) if $x < 0$ but the program is modified using the formula (13.3)? Explain why these results are obtained.*

Exercise 13.11 *If your compiler supports the rounding modes, modify Program 9 using the interval arithmetic idea. Compute lower and upper bounds on the sum, using* round down *and* round up. *You may have to change the termination condition in order to avoid an infinite loop; why? How well do the lower and upper bounds agree when $x = 10$? How well do they agree when $x = -10$? Can you also get lower and upper bounds for the result computed by the stable version of the algorithm incorporating (13.3)? (This requires thought; see Exercise 10.18.) Do you conclude that the rounding modes are useful for testing the stability of an algorithm?*

Exercise 13.12 *Write a stable modification of Program 9 that computes the function $\exp(x) - 1$ without any calls to the math library. Compare your answer with the result computed by* expm1 *(see Exercise 13.4).*

Exercise 13.13 *It is well known that the harmonic series*

$$1 + \frac{1}{2} + \frac{1}{3} + \frac{1}{4} + \cdots$$

does not converge. Write a C program to sum this series, using Program 9 as a model, terminating if the sum is unchanged by the addition of a term. Use an integer n *to control the loop but compute the terms of the series as the floating point expression* 1.0/n, *not the integer expression* 1/n, *which rounds down to zero for* n > 1. *Use* float *variables, not* double. *Does the program terminate? Including a print statement in the loop will greatly slow down program execution.*

Exercise 13.14 *If you have a fast computer with nothing much to do, modify the program for Exercise 13.13 to use double precision. Do not include a print statement in the loop. This time, you will find that the value of* n *runs through all* $2^{31} - 1$ *positive integers until integer overflow occurs. Then what happens? If the overflow is simply ignored, the loop continues to run through all* 2^{31} *negative integers as well, in reverse order, until finally, at step* 2^{32} *of the loop, all bits of the result become zero (the overflow bit which does not fit the 32-bit word is discarded). Since* n *is now zero, the floating point value for the term* 1.0/n *becomes* ∞, *the sum becomes* ∞, *and the loop terminates the next time through, when* n *is 1 and the sum is still* ∞. *So we get the right answer (that the series diverges to* ∞*) for* completely the wrong reason*! Unfortunately, C99 did not impose requirements on system response to integer overflow.*

Exercise 13.15 *It is well known that the series*

$$1 + \frac{1}{4} + \frac{1}{9} + \frac{1}{16} + \cdots$$

converges to $\pi^2/6$. *Write a C program to sum this series, terminating if the sum is unchanged by the addition of a term. How good are the results using single precision? Using double precision? Use an integer* n *to control the loop but assign this to a* float *variable before you square it, to avoid integer overflow.*

Exercises 13.13 through 13.15 show that it is not always easy to write a stable algorithm to sum a series. See [Hig96, Section 1.12.4 and Chapter 4] for more details.

Interval Arithmetic and Arbitrary Precision Arithmetic

Interval arithmetic and arbitrary precision arithmetic are two approaches that are useful to users whose applications require a guaranteed accuracy and who are willing to pay the price of slower execution to achieve their goals. A working of Exercises 10.17, 10.18, 13.5, and 13.11 demonstrates both the power and the limitations of interval arithmetic. The power is that guaranteed lower and upper bounds on the desired solution are computed, but the limitation is that these bounds may not be close together, especially if the problem being solved is ill conditioned. It should be clear from a working of the exercises that carrying out a complicated calculation with interval arithmetic would be very clumsy with only the rounding modes as tools. However, software packages are available that carry out interval computations automatically. INTLAB [Rum] is an efficient and powerful MATLAB toolbox for interval arithmetic.

Arbitrary precision systems make computations to arbitrarily high precision. These come in several flavors. The traditional approach is to carry out all computations using a prescribed precision, i.e., a prescribed number of significand bits or digits. Since no computer provides hardware support for this, such systems must be implemented in software, typically using an array of integers to represent the consecutive significand bits of a "big" floating point number. Operations on such numbers would traditionally be implemented using the integer arithmetic hardware operations. Systems of this kind are provided, for example, by the symbolic packages *Mathematica* and *Maple* (the latter also available via MATLAB's symbolic toolbox), and by the Unix tool dc. Such systems do not provide any guarantees on the accuracy of the final results. Regardless

CHAPTER 13. STABILITY OF ALGORITHMS

of how many precision bits are in use, if a problem is sufficiently ill-conditioned, the computed solution will have no significant digits. When the goal is to provide results with guaranteed accuracy, some sort of adaptive precision must be used.

During the past decade, there has been a shift toward using floating point hardware operations to implement high precision algorithms. This development has been driven partly by the widespread acceptance of the IEEE standard, ensuring correctly rounded results, and partly by the highly optimized performance of floating point hardware operations on most microprocessors. In such systems, a number x is represented by an array of k IEEE floating point numbers $y_1, \ldots, y_k$, where $k \geq 2$. The value of x represented by this array is the sum $y_1 + \cdots + y_k$. If $k = 2$ and y_1 and y_2 are both IEEE double format numbers, this system is called *double double*. For example, the number $2^{100} + 2^{-1000}$ can be represented exactly as a *double double*, since both 2^{100} and 2^{-1000} are IEEE double format numbers. Arithmetic operations on numbers of this kind are provided by routines that perform a relatively small number of hardware floating point operations [Pri91, She97]. If guaranteed accuracy is required for the final result, k must be allowed to increase as the computation progresses. See [LD+02] for recent work on extending the BLAS (Basic Linear Algebra Subroutines) to high precision, as well as much information about various current approaches to extended and arbitrary precision computation. ARPREC [BH+02] is a state-of-the-art arbitrary precision package that builds on the *double double* idea.

Arbitrary precision arithmetic may be needed when the answer required is actually a discrete quantity, such as a yes/no answer. For example, in computational geometry, it may be necessary to know whether or not a given point is inside a circle determined by three other points (an ill-conditioned problem when the points are nearly collinear). The algorithms of [She97] are motivated by this application, and give results with guaranteed accuracy for a certain class of problems.

However, arbitrary precision is not a panacea. It is impractical in large scale scientific computing since it is so much slower than double precision. It may be misleading if, as is often the case, the data input to the computation are not known exactly. Furthermore, the problem being solved may have other sources of errors, e.g., discretization errors, that are far more significant than rounding errors. As Trefethen says [Tre97, p. 324], "Floating point arithmetic is a name for numerical analysts' habit of pruning [the accuracy of the computation] at every step along the way of a calculation rather than in a single act at the end." He was making a comparison between numerical and symbolic computation, but the same observation applies here.

As technology advances, so do users' requirements and expectations. The ongoing revision of the IEEE standard [IEE-R] addresses the issue of 128-bit quadruple precision floating point formats; at present, hardware support for quadruple precision is provided only by IBM 390 processors. Inevitably, 256-bit floating point will become standard eventually. Equally inevitably, there will be some users for whom this will not be enough, who will use arbitrary precision algorithms.

Chapter 14

Conclusion

Here is a summary of some of the most important ideas in this book.

- Floating point representation of numbers is ubiquitous in numerical computing, since fixed point numbers have very restricted ranges. Floating point uses exponential notation, storing a sign, an exponent, and a significand in each floating point word.
- The range of possible values for IEEE single format floating point numbers is from tiny (approximately 10^{-38}) to huge (approximately 10^{38}). In addition, there are the corresponding range of negative numbers, the subnormal numbers, and the special numbers 0 and $\pm\infty$. NaN is used for the result of invalid operations. Double format numbers have a much greater finite range.
- Floating point numbers are inherently accurate only to a certain number of bits or digits. In the case of the IEEE single format, numbers have 24-bit significands, corresponding to approximately 7 significant decimal digits, and in the case of the double format, 53-bit significands, corresponding to approximately 16 significant decimal digits. Theorem 5.1 says that, when p-bit significands are in use, the rounded value of a number x satisfies

$$\text{round}(x) = x(1+\delta), \quad \text{where} \quad |\delta| < 2^{-(p-1)},$$

with $|\delta| < 2^{-p}$ when the rounding mode is *round to nearest*. The quantity $|\delta|$ is called the relative rounding error and its size depends only on the precision p of the floating point system and not on the size of x. The absolute rounding error $|x - \text{round}(x)|$ does depend on the size of x, since the gap between floating point numbers is larger for larger numbers. These results apply to normalized numbers. Subnormal numbers are less accurate. Because of its greater precision, the double format is preferred for most scientific computing applications.

- One floating point arithmetic operation is required, under the rules of the IEEE standard, to give the exact result rounded correctly using the relevant rounding mode and precision. Such a result is by definition accurate to 24 bits (about 7 digits) when the destination format is IEEE single, and to 53 bits (about 16 digits) when the destination format is IEEE double, unless the number is subnormal. Exceptional cases may yield a result equal to $\pm\infty$ or NaN.
- A sequence of floating point operations generally does not give correctly rounded exact results. Furthermore, one cannot expect the results to be accurate to 7 significant digits (or 16 digits when the double format is in use). Accuracy of computations is limited by the condition number of the problem being solved. Rule of Thumb 12.1 says that the number of significant digits in the computed results can be expected to be, at best, about 7 minus the base 10 logarithm of the condition number (or 16 minus the base 10 logarithm of the condition number if the double format is in use).

- A stable algorithm is one that solves a problem to approximately the accuracy predicted by Rule of Thumb 12.1. A poor choice of algorithm may give much worse results; in this case the algorithm is said to be unstable. This may happen because of cancellation or, more generally, because of intermediate steps that introduce ill conditioning.

Numerical Algorithms and Numerical Analysis

In this book, we have not even begun to discuss algorithms for the solution of nontrivial numerical problems, nor the analysis that underlies them. Many fine books, old and new, contain a wealth of information on these most classical of scientific subjects. Numerical algorithms and analysis form such a fundamental part of computer science and applied mathematics that Knuth, in the preface to his celebrated multivolume series *The Art of Computer Programming*, commented that his subject might be called "nonnumerical analysis" [Knu68]. He felt this was too negative, so he suggested instead "analysis of algorithms," a name that stuck.

We cannot list more than a tiny fraction of the many books on numerical algorithms and analysis, but we mention a few favorite books, all published since 1995 (a sign that the subject is thriving). Good choices to begin with are [Hea02, Ste96, Van00]. For a more comprehensive introduction, with extensive discussion of computer architecture and software not found in most books, see [Ueb97]. For linear algebra, see [Dem97, Hig96, TB97]. For differential equations, see [AP98, Ise96]. For optimization, see [NW99]. For statistics, see [Lan99].

Numerical analysis is, according to Trefethen [Tre97, p. 323], the study of algorithms for the problems of continuous mathematics—*not* just the study of rounding errors. We completely agree. As Trefethen says, "The central mission of numerical analysis is to compute quantities that are typically uncomputable, from an analytical point of view, and do it with lightning speed." Floating point computing is the workhorse that makes this possible.

Reliability Is Paramount

There is one thing that is even more important than lightning speed, and that is reliability. This applies to all kinds of computing and is an issue that received extensive publicity in the late 1990's because of Year 2000 conversions.

As Kahan says, speed should not be confused with throughput [Kah00]. Fast programs that break down occasionally and therefore require a lot of user interaction may be less useful than highly reliable, slower programs. Floating point hardware operations have become both very fast and, thanks in large part to the IEEE standard, very reliable. Although the computer industry has, by and large, been hugely supportive of the IEEE standard, there are still some unfortunate holes in that support. The most serious is that some microprocessors implement gradual underflow and subnormal arithmetic only in software. Although this is permitted by the standard, the result is that Fortran and C compiler writers, for whom speed is paramount, offer "fast" options that disable gradual underflow and subnormal numbers and flush all underflowed values to zero. One problem that this creates is that heterogeneous networks of workstations, some of which support gradual underflow in hardware and some only in software, cannot reliably pass data to each other if they are all running in "fast" mode because subnormal numbers would be invalid on some machines [Dem00]. Let us hope that a critical program somewhere is not relying on a *yes* answer to Question 6.4 while running in a "fast" mode, because the answer may be *no* when subnormal values are not permitted. Hopefully, when people in the future look back on the current technology of often-disabled software-supported gradual underflow, with its implication of a possible *no* answer to Question 6.4, they will find it as archaic as we now see many of the anomalies of the 1960s and 1970s, such as possible *no* answers to Questions 6.1 through 6.3.

We conclude by noting that loss of precision in floating point computation can have unexpectedly serious consequences. During the 1991 Gulf War, the United States used a missile defense system called Patriot to defend its troops. On one occasion, the system failed badly, and an analysis after the event explained what happened. The internal clock of the computer that controlled the defense system stored the time as an integer value in units of tenths of a second, and the computer program converted this to a floating point value in units of seconds, rounding the expansion (2.3) accordingly. Because the program was an old one that had been updated to account for new technology, the conversion to floating point was done more accurately in some places in the program than in others. To calculate a time interval, the program took two snapshots of the clock and subtracted them. Because of the rounding inconsistencies, the system failed to work when it had been running for more than 100 hours [Ske92].

Floating point to integer conversion can also cause catastrophic errors if the conversion overflows the integer format and appropriate recovery is not made. It was an error of this kind that triggered the destruction of Ariane 5, the European Space Agency's billion-dollar rocket, in June 1996. Thirty-seven seconds after liftoff, a program tried to convert the rocket's horizontal velocity from a double format to a short integer format. The number in question was easily within the normalized range of the double floating point format, but was too big for the 16-bit short integer format. When the invalid operation occurred, the program, instead of taking some appropriate action, shut down the entire guidance system and the rocket self-destructed [Inq96]. The same floating point to integer conversion issue arose again with the discovery of a bug in the Pentium Pro and Pentium II microprocessors in April 1997. However, the Ariane bug was a software bug, while the Pentium II bug was a hardware bug: the invalid operation status flag that was supposed to be set when overflow took place, according to IEEE standard specifications, was not in fact set. Intel handled this bug much more professionally than the Pentium division bug, which the company had attempted to cover up; as a result, the bug was fixed fairly promptly and without much controversy.

In the modern world, many critical matters are dependent on complex computer programs, from air traffic control systems to heart machines. Many of these codes depend, in one way or another, on floating point computing.

Bibliography

[App88]   *Apple Numerics Manual.* Addison-Wesley, Reading, MA, Menlo Park, CA, second edition, 1988.

[AP98]   U. M. Ascher and L. R. Petzold. *Computer Methods for Ordinary Differential Equations and Differential-Algebraic Equations*, SIAM, Philadelphia, 1998.

[BH+02]   D. H. Bailey, Y. Hida, X.S. Li and B Thompson. ARPREC: An arbitrary precision computation package, 2002. http://crd.lbl.gov/~dbailey/dhbpapers/arprec.pdf

[Cha79]   A. B. Chace. *The Rhind Mathematical Papyrus.* National Council of Teachers of Mathematics, Reston, VA, 1979. The cited quote is from Volume 1, pp. 48–49.

[Cla99]   Arthur C. Clarke. *2001: A Space Odyssey.* New American Library, Penguin Putnam, New York, 1999. Based on a screenplay by Stanley Kubrick and Arthur C. Clarke, 1968.

[CKVV02] A. Cuyt, P. Kuterna, B. Verdonk and D. Verschaeren. Underflow revisited. *Calculo*, 39(3):169-179, 2002.

[Cod81]   W. J. Cody. Analysis of proposals for the floating-point standard. *Computer*, 14(3):63–69, 1981.

[Coo81]   J. T. Coonen. Underflow and the denormalized numbers. *Computer*, 14(3):75–87, 1981.

[Dar98]   J.D. Darcy. *Borneo: adding IEEE 754 support to Java.* M.S. thesis, University of California, 1998. http://www.jddarcy.org/Borneo/borneo.pdf

[Dem84]   J. W. Demmel. Underflow and the reliability of numerical software. *SIAM J. Sci. Stat. Comput.*, 5:887–919, 1984.

[Dem91]   J. W. Demmel. On the odor of IEEE arithmetic. *NA Digest*, 91(39) Sept. 29, 1991. http://www.netlib.org/na-digest-html/91/v91n39.html#15

[Dem97]   J. W. Demmel. *Applied Numerical Linear Algebra.* SIAM, Philadelphia, 1997.

[Dem00]   J. W. Demmel, 2000. Private communication.

[DL94]   J. W. Demmel and X. Li. Faster numerical algorithms via exception handling. *IEEE Trans. Comput.*, 43:983–992, 1994.

[Ede97]   A. Edelman. The mathematics of the Pentium division bug. *SIAM Review*, 39:54–67, 1997.

[Ede94]   A. Edelman. When is $x * (1/x) \neq 1$?, 1994.
http://www.math.mit.edu/~edelman

[Fig00]   S. Figueroa. *A Rigorous Framework for Fully Supporting the IEEE Standard for Floating-Point Arithmetic in High-Level Programming Languages*. Ph.D. thesis, New York University, 2000.
http://www.cs.nyu.edu/csweb/Research/theses.html

[Gay90]   D. M. Gay. Correctly rounded binary-decimal and decimal-binary conversions. Technical report, 1990, AT&T Bell Labs Numerical Analysis Manuscript 90-10. http://www.ampl.com/REFS/rounding.ps.gz

[Gol91]   D. Goldberg. What every computer scientist should know about floating-point arithmetic. *ACM Computer Surveys*, 23:5–48, 1991.

[Gol95]   D. Goldberg. *Computer Arithmetic*. Kaufmann, San Mateo, CA, second edition, 1995. Appendix in [HP95].

[Hea02]   M. T. Heath. *Scientific Computing: An Introductory Survey*. McGraw-Hill, New York, second edition, 2002.

[HP95]   J. L. Hennessy and D. L. Patterson. *Computer Architecture: A Quantitative Approach*. Kaufmann, San Mateo, CA, second edition, 1995.

[HH00]   D. J. Higham and N. J. Higham. *MATLAB Guide*. SIAM, Philadelphia, 2000.

[Hig96]   N. J. Higham. *Accuracy and Stability of Numerical Algorithms*. SIAM, Philadelphia, 1996.

[Hou81]   D. Hough. Applications of the proposed IEEE 754 standard for floating-point arithmetic. *Computer*, 14(3):70–74, 1981.

[IEE85]   IEEE standard for binary floating-point arithmetic: ANSI/IEEE std 754-1985, 1985. Reprinted in *SIGPLAN Notices* 22(2):9–25, 1987.
http://grouper.ieee.org/groups/754/

[IEE87]   IEEE standard for radix-independent floating-point arithmetic: ANSI/IEEE Std 854-1987, 1987. http://grouper.ieee.org/groups/754/

[IEE-R]   IEEE 754 Revision Work. http://grouper.ieee.org/groups/754/revision.html

[Inq96]   Inquiry board traces Ariane 5 failure to overflow error. *SIAM News*, 29(8), Oct. 1996, pp. 1, 12, 13.
http://www.siam.org/siamnews/general/ariane.htm

[Ise96]   A. Iserles. *A First Course in the Numerical Analysis of Differential Equations*. Cambridge University Press, Cambridge (UK), New York, 1996.

[ISO99]   ISO/IEC 9899:1999 Standard for the C programming language (C99), 1999.
http://www.iso.ch/. January 1999 draft available at
http://anubis.dkuug.dk/JTC1/SC22/WG14/www/docs/n869/

[Jav]   Java Numerics. http://math.nist.gov/javanumerics/

BIBLIOGRAPHY

[Kah96a] W. Kahan. The baleful effect of computer benchmarks upon applied mathematics, physics and chemistry, 1996.
http://www.cs.berkeley.edu/~wkahan/ieee754status/baleful.ps

[Kah96b] W. Kahan. Lecture notes on the status of IEEE standard 754 for binary floating-point arithmetic, 1996.
http://www.cs.berkeley.edu/~wkahan/ieee754status/ieee754.ps

[Kah97] W. Kahan. The John von Neumann lecture at the SIAM 45th annual meeting, 1997.
http://www.cs.berkeley.edu/~wkahan/SIAMjvnl.ps

[Kah98] W. Kahan and J.D. Darcy. How Java's floating-point hurts everyone everywhere, 1998. http://www.cs.berkeley.edu/~wkahan/JAVAhurt.pdf

[Kah00] W. Kahan. Ruminations on the design of floating-point arithmetic, 2000.
http://www.cs.nyu.edu/cs/faculty/overton/book/docs/KahanTalk.pdf

[Knu68] D. E. Knuth. *The Art of Computer Programming, Volume 1: Fundamental Algorithms*. Addison-Wesley, Reading, MA, 1968.

[Knu98] D. E. Knuth. *The Art of Computer Programming, Volume 2: Seminumerical Algorithms*. Addison-Wesley, Reading, MA, third edition, 1998.

[Lan99] K. Lange, *Numerical Analysis for Statisticians*, Springer, New York, 1999.

[LD+02] X. Li, J. Demmel, D. Bailey, G. Henry, Y. Hida, J. Iskandar, W. Kahan, S. Y. Kang, A. Kapur, M. C. Martin, B. J. Thompson, T. Tung and D. J. Yoo. Design, implementation, and testing of extended and mixed precision BLAS. *ACM Trans. Math. Software*, 28:152–163, 2002.

[MRC04] M. Metcalf, J. Reid and M. Cohen. *Fortran 95/2003 Explained*. Oxford University Press, Oxford, 2004.

[MHR80] N. Metropolis, J. Howlett, and G.-C. Rota, editors. *A History of Computing in the Twentieth Century*. Academic Press, New York, 1980.

[Mul97] J.-M. Muller. *Elementary Functions: Algorithms and Implementation*. Birkhaüser, Boston, Basel, Berlin, 1997.

[Net] Netlib. http://www.netlib.org

[NW99] J. Nocedal and S. J. Wright. *Numerical Optimization*. Springer, New York, 1999.

[PH97] D. L. Patterson and J. L. Hennessy. *Computer Organization and Design: the Hardware/Software Interface*. Kaufmann, San Mateo, CA, second edition, 1997.

[Pri91] D. M. Priest. Algorithms for arbitrary precision floating point arithmetic. In P. Kornerup and D. Matula, editors, *Proceedings of the 10th Symposium on Computer Arithmetic*, pp. 132–143, Piscataway, NJ, 1991. IEEE Computer Society Press.

[Rob95] E. S. Roberts. *The Art and Science of C*. Addison-Wesley Reading, MA, Menlo Park, CA, 1995.

[Rum]	S. M. Rump. INTLAB: Interval Laboratory, a MATLAB toolbox for interval arithmetic. http://www.ti3.tu-harburg.de/rump/intlab/
[Sev98]	C. Severance. An interview with the old man of floating-point: Reminiscences elicited from William Kahan, 1998. http://www.cs.berkeley.edu/~wkahan/ieee754status/754story.html A condensed version appeared in *Computer*, 31:114–115, 1998.
[She97]	J. R. Shewchuk. Adaptive precision floating-point arithmetic and fast robust geometric predicates. *Discrete Comput. Geom.*, 18(3):305–363, 1997. http://www.cs.cmu.edu/~quake/robust.html
[Ske92]	R. Skeel. Roundoff error and the Patriot missile. *SIAM News*, 25(4), July 1992, p. 11. http://www.siam.org/siamnews/general/patriot.htm
[Ste74]	P. Sterbenz, *Floating Point Computation*, Prentice-Hall, Englewood Cliffs, NJ, 1974.
[Ste96]	G. W. Stewart. *Afternotes on Numerical Analysis*. SIAM, Philadelphia, 1996.
[TB97]	L. N. Trefethen and D. Bau, III. *Numerical Linear Algebra*. SIAM, Philadelphia, 1997.
[Tre97]	L. N. Trefethen. The definition of numerical analysis. In [TB97], pp. 321–327.
[Ueb97]	C. W. Ueberhuber. *Numerical Computation: Methods, Software, and Analysis*. Springer-Verlag, Berlin, New York, 1997. Two volumes.
[Van00]	C. Van Loan. *Introduction to Scientific Computing: A matrix-vector approach using MATLAB*. Prentice-Hall, Upper Saddle River, NJ, second edition, 2000.
[Web96]	*Webster's New World College Dictionary*. Macmillan, New York, 1996.
[Wil64]	J. H. Wilkinson. *Rounding Errors in Algebraic Processes*. Prentice-Hall, Englewood Cliffs, NJ, 1964. Reprinted by Dover, New York, 1994.
[Wil85]	M. R. Williams. *A History of Computing Technology*. Prentice-Hall, Englewood Cliffs, NJ, 1985.
[Wil98]	M. V. Wilkes. A revisionist account of early language development. *Computer*, 31:22–26, 1998.
[WW92]	D. Weber-Wulff. Rounding error changes parliament makeup. *The Risks Digest*, 13(37), 1992. http://catless.ncl.ac.uk/Risks/13.37.html#subj4
[Zus93]	K. Zuse. *The Computer—My Life*. Springer-Verlag, Berlin, New York, 1993.

Index

−0, 18, 26, 43, 67
2's complement, 9, 10
∞, 18, 27, 42, 46, 65–67, 69

absolute rounding error, 27, 44, 62, 63, 97
Apple, 49, 56
arbitrary precision, 94, 95
Ariane, 99

Babbage, Charles, 1
Big Endian, 24, 61
BInary to decimal conversion, 59
binary to decimal conversion, 39

C, 55–70
cancellation, 35, 71–75, 88, 92, 98
central difference quotient, 75
Colossus, 2
complex arithmetic, 57
compound interest, 84–88
condition number, 78–84, 86, 88, 93, 97
Cray, 36

DEC, 18, 24, 49
decimal to binary conversion, 39, 59
denormalized, *see* subnormal
difference quotient, 72–74, 82, 88
discretization error, 74, 75, 95
division by zero, 11, 18, 41–46, 65, 69
double double, 95
double precision, *see* IEEE double format

ENIAC, 2
exception, 41–47
exception masks, 52, 57
exponent bias, 20, 22
extended precision, *see* arbitrary precision, IEEE extended format

fixed point, 11, 16
floating point, 11ff.
Fortran, 55–57, 98

fused multiply-add, 52–53, 66

gradual underflow, 44, 45, 62, 98, 99
guard bit, 35, 36

hidden bit, 12–15, 18, 19, 23, 37

IBM, 17, 24, 36, 49, 53, 55
IEEE double format, 22f.
IEEE extended format, 23, 33, 49, 56–57
IEEE p754, 17
IEEE single format, 19ff.
Intel, 18, 23, 38, 49–53, 57, 64, 93, 99
interval arithmetic, 34, 68, 88, 93, 94
invalid operation, 42–46, 51, 97, 99

Java, 55–57

Kahan, William, 17, 18, 51, 56, 67

Little Endian, 24, 61

machine epsilon, 14, 15, 23, 28, 29, 32, 74, 77
math library, 66, 67, 80, 87, 88
MATLAB, 57, 94
Moler, Cleve, 18

NaN, 19, 20, 22, 42–46, 51, 56, 67, 72, 79, 97
Napier, John, 1
negative zero, *see* −0
Netlib, 55
Newton, Isaac, 1, 38
N_{max}, 20, 22, 25–28, 46, 69
N_{min}, 20, 22, 25–29, 46, 62
normalization, 12, 17, 21, 34
normalized, 12–23, 25, 34–35
normalized range, 25–29, 32, 46, 56, 71, 77, 78, 83, 99
numerical analysis, 98

overflow, 44–46, 50, 68, 69, 93

    integer, 10, 11, 94, 99
    stack, 51, 52

Palmer, John, 18
Patriot, 99
positional number systems, 6
precision, 14ff.
precision mode, 50, 52, 56, 57

register stack, 50, 51
relative rounding error, 28, 45, 77, 78, 97
remainder, 31, 38, 43
round down, 26–28, 34, 68, 93
round to nearest, 27–29ff.
round towards zero, 27, 28
round up, 26–28, 33–35, 64, 66, 68, 93
rounding mode, 26–29, 31–34, 37, 39, 52, 56, 62, 63, 68, 77, 94, 97
Rule of Thumb, 78, 80, 81, 97, 98

significand, 12–16ff.
significant digits, 23, 24, 29, 60, 61, 64, 74, 79, 86, 88, 92, 93, 97
single precision, *see* IEEE single format
square root, 38, 43, 57, 66, 68, 74
stable, 83, 87, 88, 93, 94, 98
standard response, 41–44, 46, 51, 56, 57, 65, 69, 93
status flag, 46, 52, 56, 57, 69, 99
sticky bit, 36
subnormal, 19–21, 23, 25, 26, 44, 45, 62, 70, 97, 98
Sun, 23, 24, 49, 55, 57

Turing, Alan, 2
two's complement, 9, 10

ulp, 14, 27, 66, 67
underflow, 44, 46, 62, 67–70, 89, 98, 99
unstable, 83, 84, 86–88, 92, 93, 98

von Neumann, John, 2, 16

Wilkes, Maurice, 2, 55
Wilkinson, James, 2, 16

Zuse, Konrad, 2